Culturally
Proficient
Learning
Communities

*In memory of my parents, Vic and Lois Broom, for their
many years of community service.*

—Delores

*To Gary, my husband, for bringing joy and balance to our lives, while continually
nurturing and supporting my personal and professional learning.*

—Linda

*To Momma and Daddy, who valued education so much that they sent themselves and their
five children to university, creating and opening doors to the future for each of us.*

—Jarvis

To Harry Babbitt for his showing me the way.

—Randy

Delores B. Lindsey
Linda D. Jungwirth
Jarvis V. N. C. Pahl
Randall B. Lindsey
Foreword by Shirley M. Hord

Culturally Proficient Learning Communities

Confronting
Inequities
Through
Collaborative
Curiosity

CORWIN
A SAGE Company

For information:

Corwin
A SAGE Company
2455 Teller Road
Thousand Oaks, California 91320
(800) 233-9936
Fax: (800) 417-2466
www.corwinpress.com

SAGE Ltd.
1 Oliver's Yard
55 City Road
London EC1Y 1SP
United Kingdom

SAGE India Pvt. Ltd.
B 1/I 1 Mohan Cooperative
   Industrial Area
Mathura Road, New Delhi 110 044
India

SAGE Asia-Pacific Pte. Ltd.
33 Pekin Street #02-01
Far East Square
Singapore 048763

Printed in the United States of America.

Library of Congress Cataloging-in-Publication Data

Culturally proficient learning communities : confronting inequities through collaborative curiosity/Delores B. Lindsey . . . [et al.]; foreword by Shirley M. Hord.
      p. cm.
Includes bibliographical references and index.
ISBN 978-1-4129-7227-7 (cloth : alk. paper)
ISBN 978-1-4129-7228-4 (pbk. : alk. paper)
    1. Education—Demographic aspects—United States. 2. Educational equalization—United States. 3. Multicultural education—United States.
I. Lindsey, Delores B. II. Title.

LC69.C85 2009
379.2'60973—dc22   2009010947

This book is printed on acid-free paper.

    10   11   12   13   10   9   8   7   6   5   4   3

Acquisitions Editor:	Dan Alpert
Associate Editor:	Megan Bedell
Production Editor:	Eric Garner
Copy Editor:	Jenifer Dill
Typesetter:	C&M Digitals (P) Ltd.
Proofreader:	Susan Schon
Indexer:	Terri Corry
Cover Designer:	Rose Storey

Contents

Foreword

Professional learning communities (PLCs) are everywhere—at least, that is, if one is to believe the nomenclature that many educational organizations are wearing. Some of these groups of educators meet as grade-level teams or as subject-matter departments in their schools to plan for next week's activities, some meet to divide and share the managerial tasks that accompany teaching. Some meet to devise and carry out collaborative projects. Some just meet, without identification of an agenda or any expectations for what will take place in the meeting. There are widespread operational variations or patterns that characterize PLCs. This is not unusual when a new idea or concept hits the streets.

While such variations are commonplace, they do not meet the research-based attributes that qualify a group as a PLC or the sense-making definition that the words of the PLC provide:

Professional = Who. Those in the school or district (or other organization) who share a codified body of knowledge, who operate with a specific code of ethics, and who are certified to engage in the work of the profession (e.g., teaching and learning).

Learning = Why. The purpose is to enhance and extend the learning of the membership in order to be more effective in its work with students.

Community = How. The membership of the particular group convenes itself, using democratic principles, for a specific and shared purpose.

This is an initial criterion that may be applied to ascertain if a community, or group, may be identified as an authentic PLC.

There comes a new variation of PLC that meets the three-word definition and also operates in concert with the five components identified in the research that qualify an effective PLC. These components are

1. shared beliefs, values, and vision, where the prominent attention on and value of student learning guides the community in its work;

2. shared and supportive leadership, exemplified by the sharing of power, authority, and decision making by all members;

3. supportive conditions that include *structural factors*, such as time, space, resources, policies; and *relational factors* that support high regard and respect across the membership and, in addition, caring attitudes, openness, and truth telling;

4. intentional collective learning and its application, where the community determines what it needs to learn in relationship with student needs, and how they will learn it; and

5. shared personal practice, as community members give and receive feedback on their practice, leading to individual and organizational improvement.

The PLC of attention in this book comes with a focus tailored to support the community in its study of a specific topic—a topic that the participants themselves (as is typical of an authentic PLC) have determined is essential for their knowledge, understanding, and skills so that they teach effectively and all students learn well. This is the *culturally proficient* learning community, whose genesis and development have been thoughtfully supported and encouraged by scholar/practitioners Lindsey, Jungwirth, Pahl, and Lindsey.

The members of these PLCs understand that the purpose of schools is student learning and that student learning is most significantly influenced by quality teaching. Further, they recognize and acknowledge that quality teaching is enhanced and expanded by continuous professional learning, and that this adult learning is most productive in PLC settings or environments.

While the original PLC concept never intended to dictate the content or attention of a PLC, indicating a community-specific focus appears quite appropriate. The focus on culture, in this case, makes abundant good sense given the urgent need for professional staff to serve an increasingly diverse student body. Because this area has not typically been well examined by classroom professionals, it is timely to have a product that can aid in such an exploration.

Our nation has, generally, determined that its educational system will comprehensively support students across all social and economic strata and address the specific learning needs of *all* students inclusive of their cultural or linguistic backgrounds. Further, our well meaning educators bring to the classroom their own self-defining cultural attributes, as well as their prejudices and biases. How to accommodate for the frequently wide variation in values and beliefs present and operational in classrooms?

The work suggested by authors Lindsey, Jungwirth, Pahl, and Lindsey addresses this challenge. They enlighten us about the need for exploring issues of culture in our schools. They provide us the opportunities to resolve the issues. Their volume guides us in looking with sensitivity, first to ourselves, so that we gain understanding and bring meaning to our own typically hidden realities. Then, with compassion, their work directs our learning to the cultural descriptors of students, their families, and others. The authors powerfully persuade us that we will become more complete human beings as well as educators when we have unveiled the elephant in the room and addressed our hidden issues of cultural differences with honesty and candor—and openness to transparency and change.

The authors argue, and rightly so, that the self-organizing, shared decision making, and supportive environment of the professional learning community is the setting in which a school staff can come to grips most productively with the cultural diversity of staff and students.

In the regular and frequent meetings of the school's staff, this community of professional learners invests in continuous study, conducted in a variety of modes, determined by the members. As they dialogue, discuss, and debate cultural topics about which they decide to study, their learning circle activities contribute to the members' feelings of acceptance, respect, and trust. The alliance of PLC structure and its habits of mind with the staff's goals of Cultural Proficiency results over time in goal attainment as members grow in their regard and caring for each other and in their undeviating focus on benefits for students.

Cultural Proficiency and professional learning community—a very sound union with profoundly important messages from Lindsey, Jungwirth, Pahl, and Lindsey.

—Shirley M. Hord, PhD
Scholar Laureate
National Staff Development Council
March, 2009

Preface

Beware! This book is intended to disturb schools. This is a book of questions, not answers. Our questions are designed to prompt your best thinking about ways to serve the needs of all students in our PK–12 schools. We provide stories, tools, and strategies to help transform your thinking and behaviors to disturb the current environment in which you and other community members focus your work. The bottom line is student success. The responsibility for student achievement rests with educators engaged with community members focused on ways to better serve our students. If educating all students is neither your interest nor your responsibility, then you can stop reading, now, and donate this book to your school's professional library. We are not suggesting your current thinking is wrong; we are suggesting that you, the reader, examine your current practice and be willing to think about this question:

In what ways might I think and behave with a community of learners to insure that all students perform at levels higher than ever before?

And this one:

What question will it take to shake up my thinking?

The disturbance for which we shamelessly advocate and intentionally practice is one approach to changing how educators do business in schools. We propose that educators working in and with communities of co-learners who view diversity and difference as assets and opportunities rather than deficits and disadvantages have greater opportunities to improve teaching and learning than those who work alone or in isolation from the larger school community.

The purpose of this book is to provide a lens through which to examine the goals, the intentions, and the progress of learning communities to which you belong or wish to develop. *Cultural Proficiency* is a frame through which team or group members view the context of their work. Cultural Proficiency is an *inside-out* approach for effective cross-cultural interactions. In other words, members of culturally proficient learning communities are willing to explore and assess their knowledge about the diversity of their communities, recognize the assumptions one makes about the cultural groups within their communities, and become more informed in order to be a more effective educator.

School leaders today are looking to professional learning communities (PLCs) as the answer to many of their questions about student achievement and school improvement. This urgency and rush toward implementing or imposing professional learning communities might cause one to ask, "If PLC is the answer, what was the question?" Many school leaders have discovered that declaring a team, or group, or entire school a PLC does not a professional learning community make. As Roland Barth (1991) said,

> We can work to change the embedded structures so that our schools become more hospitable places for student and adult learning. But little will really change unless we change ourselves. (p. 128)

Changing our attitudes, our beliefs, our behaviors, and ourselves is hard work. An easier approach is to find fault in others, assign blame, declare the work too hard, close our classroom door, and move on to something else. The metaphors of voice, song, and choir provide a way to represent the attitudes and behaviors of educators in today's context. Some schools are filled with voices who blame some teachers, some students, their parents, the school district, or current mandated programs for the low achievement scores of some students. While these voices may be loud singers of discontent these days, other voices sing in harmony about community-centered successes in reaching clearly focused goals for improved student achievement. This choir of community voices is the choir we invite you to join. Our choir members learn and practice the individual skills necessary to be a contributing member of the larger group. Our choir rehearses as a single unit focused on improving our performance. And ultimately, we perform in ways that honor our diversity and support our entire community. Our rehearsals and our performances disturb the silence and the discord in ways that invite, encourage, and challenge others to join our community choir.

This book integrates the four *Tools of Cultural Proficiency* with the tenets of professional learning communities. We provide protocols, activities, and rubrics to convene conversations about the intersection of race, ethnicity, gender, social class, sexual orientation and identity, faith, and ableness with the disparities in student achievement. The authors believe the language, the tools, and the practices of Cultural Proficiency are missing from the current literature and practices of professional learning communities. This book proposes to address this omission by explicitly framing the work of learning communities through the lens of Cultural Proficiency.

Cultural Proficiency is a mind-set, a worldview through which to examine our beliefs, values, assumptions, and behaviors. This book defines and describes culture in its broadest sense. Culture is inclusive of and involves more than ethnic or racial differences. Culture is the set of practices and beliefs that is shared with members of a particular group and that distinguishes one group from others (Lindsey, Nuri Robins, & Terrell, 2003, p. 14). Culture includes shared characteristics of human description, including race, ethnicity, age, gender, sexual orientation and identity, faith, spirituality, ableness, geography, ancestry, language, history, occupation, and affiliations.

Readers and the cowriters of this book are members of various and diverse cultural groups, and we may hold several cultural aspects in common. For example, we bring our experiences as school leaders and our work toward creating equitable schools to this writing so we may better serve the needs of all students. We have written this book for school leaders who hold a passion for equity through collaborative community development. We define school leaders as teacher leaders, site and district office administrators, counselors, staff members, parents, and other community partners. We recognize that it takes both formal and informal leaders to achieve the learning goals we set for our students and ourselves. We invite you to keep your leadership role(s) in mind as you read this book. Welcome to our journey toward culturally proficient practices.

Parts I, II, and III of this book describe the chapters' contents and offer transitions and connections for the reader. Each chapter opens with an epigraph for the reader's reflection. The chapters are formatted for the reader to get centered with prompts for thinking, go deeper with descriptions and tools, and reflect using a series of questions designed to guide the *inside-out* approach for culturally proficient practices.

Chapters 1 through 3 introduce the four Tools for Cultural Proficiency, explore the history of inequity in schools, review the current emphasis on professional learning communities, present a framework for integrating the two concepts, provide a new protocol called *breakthrough questions*, and demonstrate the practical aspects of culturally proficient learning communities through the context of the Maple View community. Chapters 4 through 9 provide voices from the field to give context and application of the tools for creating and sustaining culturally proficient learning communities.

Finally, Chapter 10 offers you an invitation for deeper thinking in order to surface your assumptions about learning communities and how those assumptions influence student achievement. The chapter offers protocols and activities to support your learning. The book concludes with a call to action.

> Warning:
>
> This book is best used when in community with others. Once the community is engaged, the system of schooling as you know it will forever be curious, disturbed, and changed.

Strong warning? We mean it to be. The authors of this book intend to shake up your thinking and disturb current systems of inequity. We invite you to join us in our journey toward equity for all students through collective curiosity.

Acknowledgments

Delores, Linda, Jarvis, and Randy greatly appreciate each other as coauthors, co-learners, and friends. We are deeply grateful for the support and encouragement of our families, friends, and colleagues—who serve as our learning communities. Jarvis acknowledges her family: "My dad, John C. Calvin, Jr., who had the determination to take a giant step out of poverty; to my mother, Callie Mae Loche Calvin, who knew before she was 10 years old that the way out of not knowing was through her love of reading about the world; to my uncle, Leroy Loche, for his gift to me to travel afar. It is because of the coauthors of this book, along with my husband, Ron Hans, my children, Mothusi and Leloba, and their curiosity and desire to experience the wonders of the world, and my sister and brother, Thelma and John III, that I believe."

We acknowledge the encouragement and support of our acquisitions editor, Dan Alpert, at Corwin. As is the case in all our books and presentations about Cultural Proficiency, we acknowledge the foundational work of Terry Cross, Kikanza Nuri Robins, Ray Terrell, and our coauthor, Randy Lindsey. We offer special appreciation to Shirley Hord for her ongoing contribution to the development of learning communities.

We are grateful to the students, teachers, counselors, administrators, staff members, parents, and community partners of many school districts and county offices of education for their commitment to creating and sustaining culturally proficient learning communities. Their real stories of successes and challenges are told through the characters in our composite vignettes of Maple View School District. We wish to express our special thanks to the following: Orange County Department of Education, Instructional Services Division;

San Marcos Elementary School; Willow Grove Elementary School; Wichita, Kansas School District; Tahoe Elementary School, Sacramento, California; and the parents, students, and administrators in Fontana, Moreno Valley, San Jacinto, and Rialto school districts. For the honesty from teachers and administrators, we would also like to thank the following secondary schools: A. B. Miller, Chaffey, Eisenhower, Fontana, Lake Elsinore, San Gorgonio, Serrano, Silverado, Redlands, Don Lugo, Seepapitso Secondary in Botswana, Kolb, Kucera, and especially, Victor Valley and Palm Springs High Schools. We also offer our thanks to Etiwanda Elementary School District; elementary schools in Rialto Unified School District, including Bemis, Boyd, Dollahan, Dunn, Fitzgerald, Henry, Kelly, Morris, and Trapp; Moreno Valley Unified School District's Sunneymead Elementary; The Center for the Advancement of Small Learning Environments (CASLE) at the San Bernardino County Superintendent of Schools; University of California, Los Angeles' School Management Program; University of Botswana's English and History Departments, and professors who had the courage to be the difference. We thank the individuals who misunderstood our intentions for a deeper cause. We thank our friends on the six continents traveled. Without you, our efforts would indeed be minimized. It is from all of you that our greatest learning occurred.

This book has been a journey of purpose and passion. We acknowledge our individual and collective commitment of time and energy and our willingness to stay true to the book we wanted to write from the very beginning.

About the Authors

Delores B. Lindsey, PhD, is Associate Professor of Educational Administration at California State University San Marcos in San Marcos, California. She is coauthor of three Corwin publications, *Culturally Proficient Instruction: A Guide for People Who Teach,* (2002, 2006), the multimedia kit by the same name, and *Culturally Proficient Coaching: Supporting Educators to Create Equitable Schools* (2007). Delores is a former middle grades and high school teacher, middle grades site administrator, and county office of education administrator. As a professor, she serves schools, districts, and county offices as Cognitive Coach Training Associate, Adaptive Schools Associate, and as a consultant to develop culturally proficient educators. Delores' favorite roles are that of "Mimi" to her grandchildren and "Dr. Punkin" to her husband, Randy.

Linda D. Jungwirth, EdD, is President of Convening Conversations, Inc., a company devoted to leading educators in courageous conversations and professional development to achieve equity and success for all students. Linda helps schools, districts, and county superintendent offices enhance their professional development with an emphasis on instructional effectiveness, cognitive coaching, and culturally proficient learning communities. As adjunct professor at Pepperdine University, she inspires educators to become culturally proficient leaders and innovators. Linda received the 2008 Association of California School Administrators (ACSA) *Wilson A. Grace Award* for her ideals of tolerance, compassion, and professional leadership, and as a leader who motivates and inspires personal and professional growth in others. Linda's favorite place is a beautiful mountainside in central Colorado. She loves golfing and hiking with her husband,

Gary, who provides balance and constant support for her many endeavors.

Jarvis V. N. C. Pahl, EdD, is Executive Director of Pahl Business & Educational Consortium (PBEC). She taught biology and microbiology in California, Maryland, Connecticut, and Brazil. She also taught while in the Peace Corps and in Botswana, Africa. As a school administrator, she worked in California high schools and school districts. She was a member of the Graduate School of Education's School Management Program at the University of California in Los Angeles. She has traveled in Asia, Africa, Europe, North America, South America, Antarctica, and the Arctic Circle. She speaks Portuguese, some Setswana (the language of Botswana), and Spanish. As a consultant, she has designed, planned, and facilitated hundreds of learning experiences for parent groups, students, teachers, administrators, blended groups of educators, parents, students, and individuals from the business world. She believes individuals have a gene for leadership in their area of specialty. Jarvis and her traveling companions, her husband and their daughter and mother (when they are available), have every intention of taking time to travel to that one continent not yet traveled, Australia. She enjoys getting people together to have fun with games that result in laughter and bringing out "the other side" we rarely experience, especially in her ninety-year-old mother who found out how to laugh when she was eighty.

Randall B. Lindsey, PhD, is Emeritus Professor, California State University Los Angeles. He is coauthor of six Cultural Proficiency books and a multimedia kit. He is coauthor with Franklin and Brenda CampbellJones of *The Cultural Proficiency Journey: Moving Beyond Our Barriers Toward Profound School Change* (publication scheduled for summer 2009). Randy is a former high school history teacher, school administrator, and staff developer on issues of school desegregation and equity. He consults and coaches school districts and universities as they develop culturally proficient leaders. Randy spends his spare time cultivating an herb garden in his San Diego County home. The herbs enrich his cooking and the garden helps Delores and him stay connected to the vital gift of life they enjoy.

PART I

Getting Centered

This book presents culturally proficient practices through the context of professional learning. We use the term *professional learning* rather than *staff development* or *professional development* because we intend to broaden the conversation beyond inservice or formal training to include all professional learning experiences in which educators engage. These experiences include, but are not limited to, assessment and inquiry-driven planning, instructional design and strategies, curriculum development, coaching, leadership development, shared decision making, and culturally proficient collaborative educational practices.

In this book, we intentionally created a focus on learning communities where all members, including students, teachers, parents, administrators, classified and certificated staff, school community members, and school partners actively create a sense of collaborative curiosity that probes deeper, long-term self-commitments and collaborative commitments to learning. This collaborative curiosity is key to developing both support and actions that result in the confrontation of inequities in schools. The intended results of actively confronting these inequities through collaborative curiosity are higher performance and growth for each and every community member.

Part I: Getting Centered is composed of Chapters 1 through 3. These chapters ground the reader in the Tools for Culturally Proficient Educational Practices as well as the history of reform and equity in North American schools. For first time readers on Cultural Proficiency, Chapter 1 serves as an introduction to the concept of Cultural Proficiency and to the Tools for Cultural Proficiency. For readers already familiar with Cultural Proficiency (Lindsey, Nuri Robins, & Terrell, 2003; Nuri Robins, Lindsey, Lindsey, & Terrell, 2006; Lindsey, Martinez, & Lindsey, 2007), this chapter can serve as a review and renewal of the approach and four tools. Chapter 1 presents a frame for integrating the Essential Elements of Cultural Proficiency with the tenets of professional learning communities.

Chapter 2 traces the evolutionary nature of equity issues in our democratic societies, such as PK–12 schools and other public institutions of learning. You will read about significant events and mandates that have shaped the policies and practices of our schools and that either facilitate or inhibit student learning. Having an understanding of our history of equity and inequity is an important step in learning how to become a culturally proficient learning community.

Chapter 3 focuses on the definitions, descriptions, and varieties of professional learning communities. We summarize and categorize various researchers' perspectives of and experiences with learning communities. Within the current context of emphasis on learning communities, we examine the opportunities and limitations of the learning community perspective with regard to demographic groups, equity, access, and diversity using the lens of Cultural Proficiency.

1

Getting Centered

The Tools of Cultural Proficiency

Most people I meet want to develop more harmonious and satis-
fying relationships—in their organizations, communities, and
personal lives. But we may not realize that this desire can only be
satisfied by partnering with new and strange allies—curiosity
and disturbance.

—Margaret Wheatley, 2001, p. 1

Getting Centered

Margaret Wheatley (2001) invites us, as educators, to give up our
certainties and rely on each other to find our way to new discoveries
and learning. She challenges us to recognize that we cannot accomplish our learning goals alone. We need each other. In today's complex educational environments, more than ever before, we need
each other. In response to this need, many educators have developed
communities of practice and learning communities. Educational
learning communities are inclusive of teachers, school administrators,
and school partners, and they come together with a deep commitment
to their professionalism and a profound clarity about the purpose of
their work through continuous study, reflection, dialogue, and learning

(Hord & Sommers, 2008). Take a few minutes to reflect on your current role as a teacher, school administrator, counselor, professional learning specialist, or a partner of the school community.

As you think about your role(s), what is your reaction to Wheatley's quote? In what ways might a community of learners help you achieve your professional goals? In your current community, who might benefit from your contributions? What do you *get* from your community? What do you *give* to your community? Are learning communities formally identified in your current context? In which learning communities are you engaged? Use the following lines to record your thoughts or ask your questions.

Parretships ae key to banee ideas oft of.

PLC's vague

In a variety of forms, learning communities have always been part of how we work in schools. What is different now is that we are intentional in creating learning communities focused on student performance and achievement. This chapter introduces you to the intersection of the Tools of Cultural Proficiency with the characteristics of professional learning communities (PLCs). *"Culturally Proficient individuals are aware of their values and beliefs about diversity and at the same time are aware of the behaviors, policies, and practices within an organization or institution"* (Lindsey et al., 2007, p. 34). Effective members of professional learning communities are aware of the inclusive nature of their community and look for opportunities to rely on the diversity of each other to create and share their vision, mission, and collective learning. The major purpose of this chapter is to present the Tools of Cultural Proficiency as a frame for communities of learners to intentionally focus on setting and reaching academic achievement goals for students who have historically not been well served by schools.

Building a Case for Culturally Proficient Learning Communities

Learning communities, recognized by various new names, are prevalent in our schools today. Some are labeled *professional learning communities*, some use the shortened and less formal *PLC*, and some are described as *small learning communities*. Others take on the names of grade levels or departments, such as the third grade or the science department learning communities. Simply put, these meetings may in fact foster learning conversations, but they do not represent the authentic work of learning communities. Please read the following vignettes, and while reading, be fully aware of your thoughts and reactions:

- A colleague enthused about a new instructional strategy that worked well in her classroom stops by your classroom to talk with you and share her experience. In the ensuing conversation, you learn how you might use the strategy she shared in your classroom. However, during the next month, you just can't seem to find time to implement the strategy.

- In your monthly grade-level or department meeting, as a faculty you are examining the overrepresentation of males in special education. Several of you are intrigued by the data and make a list of questions for which you will seek answers or resources. When you offer to join the assistant administrator and counselor with master-schedule building for next year, you are told in a whisper, "There just isn't enough time for the necessary meetings to support addressing your questions, and by the way, we must be sure our special education staff has its teaching assignments next year. We need these students and these students need our special teachers in this capacity."

- Students in your school make bigoted, insensitive comments to one another. You and your colleagues realize there are underlying issues that need to be addressed and want to engage in a schoolwide effort to study the issue with students, their parents, and staff in order to determine effective ways to respond to students and each other.

- You attend several professional development seminars or a university course to learn how to address issues of underachievement by specific demographic groups of students (e.g., African American males, girls in the sciences, English learners). The seminars and course are taught by professionals who have an instructional history of working with individuals in the same demographic group as themselves.

- Your grade-level team has decided to examine student performance data by demographic groups and agrees to focus its instructional strategies to better serve student needs.

What thoughts and feelings occurred as you read these vignettes? Take a few moments to recall your reactions. Where do you notice learning opportunities in these occurrences? Be mindful not to describe the person or the event. Only describe the learning opportunities for you as an educator or for your school. Use this space to record your thinking:

_____

_____

_____

_____

Being in or with a learning community does not guarantee improved student achievement. Culturally proficient practices help members of the learning community examine their own values and beliefs, as well as the policies and practices of their organizations, about how we interact with our students, their families, and their community. Numerous examples and opportunities for communities are found in today's schools. Educators are invited, encouraged, and assigned to work in traditional groups or teams such as department teams, grade-level teams, faculty study groups, school leadership teams, and more recent venues such as small learning communities, houses, families, and professional learning communities.

We propose that community members be willing to closely examine their own thinking, assumptions, and behaviors will, in fact, disturb their current environments by using the *inside-out* approach for culturally proficient practices to impact and significantly change student achievement, teacher performance, administrator and parent commitments, and school community involvement and support. We suggest that opportunities for *inside-out* disturbances are immediately within our reach. The following are manifestations of these intentional, *inside-out* disturbances.

- Classrooms: Individual educators are more mindful of their own values, beliefs, and behaviors. Educators pay attention to student-to-student interactions, their interactions with fellow educators, as well as their reactions to students and colleagues. Examples include the extent to which educators recognize their gaps in cultural knowledge, their reactions to student and colleague behaviors that may be cultural in nature, and the extent to which they and fellow educators are knowledgeable about the students' neighborhoods in order to develop instructional examples familiar to students.
- Workrooms: Educators' collective values, beliefs, collective optimism and efficacy, and behaviors. Examples include the

extent to which formal and informal conversation centers on the students and their parents or guardians reflected in language that views students and parents or guardians as opportunities for educators' cultural learning as opposed to using language that views students and parents or guardians as being the source of problems.

- Leadership Meetings: Administrators' and teacher leaders' demonstrated values, beliefs, and behaviors. Examples include the manner in which culture, both in terms of the school's organizational culture as well as the students' culture, is a normal component of regular meetings, including professional development meetings.
- Boardrooms: Organizational policies and practices. Ongoing examination of district and school-site policies and practices, involving all stakeholders, to insure that district and school site policies are responsive to the needs of the diversity of the community. This oversight is particularly important for schools and districts undergoing demographic shifts. Often, shifts in student demographic populations will create emergent, new adult responses that were invisible prior to the enrollment changes. It is incumbent on policymakers to demonstrate decision-making practices that align resources and services with emergent community demographics and student needs.

Each of the illustrations above represents a unique, yet familiar, context for examining and understanding ourselves as individual educators and as members of highly complex schools and school districts. Topics of equity, diversity, and access have historical contexts that are important in order for us to know and understand the value of culturally proficient practices. Chapter 2 provides you with a context for understanding the manner in which educational equity has been an unfolding reality in our organizational democracies. In the section that follows, we describe the Tools of Cultural Proficiency so that when you read Chapter 2 the rationale for culturally proficient practices in our schools is readily apparent.

Cultural Proficiency Is About Intention

Cross (1989) describes Cultural Proficiency as an *inside-out* process of personal and organizational change. Cultural Proficiency is a lens through which we frame our personal and organizational learning and develop principles to guide our personal behaviors and organizational policies and practices. As an intentional *inside-out* process,

Cultural Proficiency provides us with the opportunity to become students of our own assumptions about self, others, and the context in which we work with others. When our context is the school or a unit within a school—grade level or department—we have the opportunity to examine assumptions that have become institutionalized as policies and practices. Learning communities take us closer to personalizing and deprivatizing our practices and actions to assist us in changing the way we talk, plan, act, and engage with others different from ourselves.

This book serves as a guide in learning and changing (as necessary) your values and behaviors, the policies and practices of your school and district, and the manner in which you and your school interact with the cultural communities you serve. With this book, you have the opportunity to

- clarify your personal values, assumptions, and beliefs about providing all demographic groups of students access to high quality education,
- develop knowledge and skills in how to work with fellow educators in developing shared values for educating all demographic groups of students,
- develop knowledge and skills in creating policies and practices that align with shared values for educating all demographic groups of students, and
- choose to act differently when you acquire and develop knowledge and skills that make a difference in your life and in the lives of the members of your learning community.

This book provides real life examples of learning communities integrating the Essential Elements of Cultural Proficiency and the tenets of professional learning communities. Table 1.1 serves as a framework for understanding, analyzing, and sustaining culturally proficient learning communities.

As you examine Table 1.1, please take a holistic view of the framework. The Essential Elements of Cultural Proficiency and the tenets of professional learning communities do not exist in isolation of the other elements and tenets. We aligned the approaches—Cultural Proficiency and learning communities—as illustrations of how school leaders might integrate the elements and tenets. Unfortunately, the linear nature of the first two columns of Table 1.1 does not reflect the dynamics and interactions in which communities engage. Therefore, we added the third column to give guidance to communities as they explore opportunities to use the essential elements within the context of learning communities.

Table 1.1 A Framework for Understanding, Analyzing, and Sustaining Culturally Proficient Learning Communities

Essential Elements of Culturally Proficient Professional Learning (Inquiry, p. 78)	Elements of Learning Communities (Hord, p. 9)	Cultural Competence Characterized By
Assess culture: *Extent to which professional learning addresses cultural identity* Professional learning informs learners about their culture, the cultures of others, and the school's culture. Educational gaps are closed through appropriate uses of cultural, linguistic, learning, and communication styles.	Shared personal practice: Community members give and receive feedback that supports their individual improvement as well as that of the organization.	• Conducting individual and group assessments. • Developing peer-to-peer support toward specific goals. • Planning and facilitating intentional professional learning to improve student learning.
Value diversity: *Extent to which professional learning addresses cultural issues* Professional learning recognizes and meets the needs of multiple cultural, linguistic, learning, and communication styles.	Shared beliefs, values, and vision: Community members consistently focus on students' learning, which is strengthened by the community's learning.	• Acknowledging multiple perspectives. • Acknowledging common purpose(s). • Basing vision and actions on common assessment results.
Manage the dynamics of diversity: *Extent to which professional learning promotes and models the use of inquiry and dialogue related to multiple perspectives.* Professional learning opportunities incorporate multiple perspectives on relevant topics and build capacity for dialogue about conflict related to difference and diversity.	Shared and supportive leadership (collaboration): Administrators and community members hold shared power and authority for making decisions.	• Openly fostering discussions about race, gender, sexual orientation, socioeconomics, and faith as related to the needs of the community. • Making decision-making processes transparent and subject to change based on community needs.

(Continued)

Table 1.1 (Continued)

Essential Elements of Culturally Proficient Professional Learning (Inquiry, p. 78)	Elements of Learning Communities (Hord, p. 9)	Cultural Competence Characterized By
Adapt to diversity: *Extent to which professional learning facilitates change to meet the needs of the community* Professional learning opportunities use data to drive change to better meet the needs of a diverse community.	Supportive and shared conditions: *Structural factors provide time, facility, resources, and policies to support collaboration.* *Relational factors support the community's human and interpersonal development, openness, truth telling, and attitudes of respect and care among the members.*	• Teaching appropriate communication skills to allow for multiple voices and experiences. • Developing adaptive practices to support newcomers as well as veteran community members.
Institutionalize cultural knowledge: *Extent to which professional learning shapes policies and practices that meet the needs of diverse learners* Professional learning opportunities are encouraged, shared, and applied in classrooms and throughout the school and the community for the purpose of improving student learning.	Collective learning and generative knowledge: Community focus is on what the community determines to learn and how they will learn it in order to address students' learning needs.	• Identifying and addressing student needs by benchmarking success indicators. • Developing a continuous improvement inquiry model to assess progress toward clearly stated achievement goals.

Sources: From *Culturally Proficient Inquiry: A Lens for Identifying and Examining Educational Gaps,* by Randall Lindsey, Stephanie Graham, Chris Westphal, and Cynthia Jew, 2008, Thousand Oaks, CA: Corwin, and *Leading Professional Learning Communities: Voices From Research and Practice,* by Shirley M. Hord and William L. Sommers, 2008, Thousand Oaks, CA: Corwin.

This framework is used to guide the Maple View learning communities through the lens of Cultural Proficiency in Chapters 5 through 9. As you examine Table 1.1, what opportunities might you find for using the Essential Elements of Cultural Proficiency to enhance and deepen your professional community's learning?

Intentional Use of the Four Tools of Cultural Proficiency

Rare is the school that doesn't have in its mission statement or statement of core values a promise "to educate all students to high levels." If not those same words, similar words and sentiments abound in our schools. The problem is that those statements too often ignore the chronic underachievement of demographic groups of students. Mercifully, our current state of accountability has removed the option of continuing to ignore underachievement.

Most states in the United States, the provinces in Canada, and the U.S. government have reform efforts (e.g., the No Child Left Behind Act) that have, at least, begun to put the spotlight on chronic areas of student underachievement. Even with the many limitations that those pieces of legislation possess, they have one irrefutable common denominator: they have drawn attention to chronic underachievement that has been present for generations. It is our observation that learning communities and Cultural Proficiency provide principles and tools that we educators can use to direct our professional resources to benefit an ever widening proportion of the children and youth in our schools.

Cultural Proficiency is about serving the needs of historically underserved students within the context of serving the needs of all students. When education is delivered in a culturally proficient manner, historically underserved students gain access to educational opportunities intended to result in high academic achievement. When education is delivered in a culturally proficient manner, all students understand and value their own culture and the cultures of those around them. Concomitantly, when the educational experience is delivered in a culturally proficient manner, all educators, legislators, board members, and local business community members understand and value the culture of those around them in ways they have rarely experienced or appreciated.

In the following section, we present the definitions and descriptions of the four Tools of Cultural Proficiency. For first time readers of Cultural Proficiency, these descriptions serve as an overview of terms and tools. For many of our longtime readers of Cultural Proficiency books, this section serves as a refresher for the terms and tools.

The following are the Tools for Cultural Proficiency to guide our work:

- Overcoming the Barriers to Cultural Proficiency—the recognition that systems of historical oppression continue to exist and can be overcome by people and organizations that adapt their values, behaviors, policies, and practices to meet the needs of underserved cultural groups using the democratic means of public education.
- The Guiding Principles of Cultural Proficiency—an inclusive set of core values that identify the centrality of culture in our lives and in our society.
- The Cultural Proficiency Continuum—six points along a continuum to indicate unhealthy and healthy ways of responding to cultural difference.
- The Five Essential Elements of Cultural Competence—five standards to guide a person's values and behaviors and a school or district's policies and practices in meeting the academic needs of cultural groups.

The Tools of Cultural Proficiency are interactive and interdependent and are discussed in the sections that follow. Tables 1.2 through 1.5 provide an orientation or overview to the four tools. Chapters 5 through 9 integrate the Tools of Cultural Proficiency with learning community principles to guide you and your colleagues as you continue to improve, expand, and enhance your practice in service and support of the diverse cultures in our schools and communities.

Tool 1: Overcoming Barriers to Cultural Proficiency—The *Why* of This *Work*

Guiding Question: What gets in the way of doing our learning community work in a culturally proficient manner?

Learning communities are a forum for recognizing, discussing, and confronting the barriers to Cultural Proficiency. In Chapter 4, we discuss Hord's (1997) tenets of learning communities, which include living a common vision, learning and collaborating with others, using disaggregated achievement data, and focusing on student learning. To be successful in culturally diverse communities, it is incumbent on educators to be able to engage in meaningful dialogue about professional and institutional barriers over which they have influence or control. Table 1.2 presents the Barriers to Cultural Proficiency.

The three bulleted items in Table 1.2 can be grouped into two overlapping themes. First, the presence of any form of oppression

Table 1.2   The Barriers to Cultural Proficiency

- **Resistance to Change**—Viewing change as needing to be done by others, not by one's self
- **Systems of Oppression**—Acknowledging and recognizing that racism, sexism, ethnocentrism, and other forms of oppression are real experiences
- **A Sense of Privilege and Entitlement**—Unawareness or indifference to benefits that accrue solely by one's membership in a gender, racial, or other cultural group

(e.g., racism) means that some people are harmed by certain practices; however, the obverse that is rarely discussed is that others benefit from those same practices in ways they don't even see or acknowledge. An example or two may be appropriate. If the two of us are voting on an issue and your vote is not counted due to your gender or race, then my vote gains value. Another example is if our school curriculum represents your experiences as mainstream in its curriculum and activities and my experiences are not represented, you gain value in our school.

The second theme present in Table 1.2 is that it is the individual who has to overcome resistance to change and adapt to the access and academic needs of the communities in our school service areas. A benefit of Cultural Proficiency is that it begins with an honest approach that recognizes the challenges within our society and then uses the tools provided by our democracy to demonstrate how to serve all demographic groups equitably.

Reflection Activity

Take a moment and read the words in Table 1.2. As you read these sentences as barriers, what feelings, reactions, or thoughts occur to you? Please record your responses in the space below.

_____

_____

_____

_____

For many people, the words and phrases will appear scary and/or irritating. Some readers may respond with feeling blamed, angry, guilty, depressed, or with questions such as "But where do we go from here?" Other readers may respond by feeling validated, curious, and with questions such as "Yes, so this is my reality and what are we going to do about it?"

This book is designed to use the second tool, the Guiding Principles of Cultural Proficiency, to address the range of questions generated from the reflections on Table 1.2. The basis of the guiding principles is recognizing that the barriers are real for many people, while for others they are invisible or not recognizable.

An example of our resistance to change as educators is embodied in the current discussions about the "achievement gap." Beginning in 1971, the National Association of Educational Progress, or NAEP, (Perie, Moran, & Lutkus, 2005) has documented, and circulated widely in the education community, detailed descriptions of academic achievement gaps. However, it has taken state and national education reforms, most widely evident in the federal reauthorization of Title I of the Elementary and Secondary Education Act (ESEA), known as the No Child Left Behind Act (2002), to draw our concerted attention to the subject. The continuing presence of educational gaps is a challenge to those of us at all levels in the education community to examine why education and academic achievement gaps continue to persist among some demographic groups of our students. As a profession, we have acted as if the National Association of Educational Progress (NAEP) data does not exist. This ongoing struggle to address the inequities that are well documented is one of the barriers that gets in the way of developing democratic classrooms and schools.

Tool 2: Guiding Principles—
Guidance in Doing Our Work

Guiding Question: Are we who we say
we are as a learning community? As a school?

The Guiding Principles of Cultural Proficiency provide a set of core values used in overcoming the Barriers to Cultural Proficiency. The barriers represent intractable issues that confound systemic school reform intended to provide adequate and appropriate education to historically underserved cultural groups of students.

The Guiding Principles of Cultural Proficiency, described in Table 1.3, provide educators with an inclusive worldview that, for some, represents a paradigmatic shift in viewing other cultural groups as capable and contributing value to the educational community. These core principles become a lens through which to examine the biannual

Table 1.3   The Guiding Principles of Cultural Proficiency

- Culture is a predominant force in schools and in people's lives
- People are served in varying degrees by the dominant culture
- People have group identities and individual identities
- Diversity within cultures is vast and significant
- Each cultural group has unique cultural needs
- The best of both worlds enhances the capacity of all

NAEP reports and other similar data conclude that current educational practices are not equitable. For that reason, we recognize that some students are well served by current policies and practices, while at the same time many educators have turned a blind eye to students not well served.

Our experience has been that when school leaders talk about *change,* they describe modifications in the structures, patterns, and processes of educational practice. Structural changes, such as revising school calendars and grade-level or department configurations, that focus on targeted demographic groups of students or that require updated professional training have the potential to change educational practices and thereby improve services for some students. However, the intent of Cultural Proficiency is to use interventions such as structural changes as a first step in a well-planned effort to transform the social and cultural conditions within schools that have a diverse student population and/or interact with a diverse community. The six Guiding Principles of Cultural Proficiency offer a pathway of additional steps for leaders as they shift their perspective on change from *reforming* structures, policies, and rules in schools to *transforming* relationships, interactions, and the behaviors of the people within schools and districts.

Those who embrace the reform perspective concentrate their efforts on how to change structures and policies. The reform perspective too often flows from a predictable mission statement that espouses goals that are not reflective of the authentic day-to-day practices of people in the school. A commonplace mission statement purports that *All students will achieve at high levels;* however, in practice this espoused goal ignores the fact that many students from identifiable demographic groups are not achieving well and haven't been for several years. In not having an authentic mission statement, schools with a reform perspective resort to default mission statements with a core belief that some students *cannot* or *will not* be well served.

The school leader who holds a transformational perspective focuses on *leadership and educational practices to meet the generative opportunities and needs of diverse communities.* Leaders engaged in transformational activities build on the experiences of the communities in their school service area. These leaders direct their own leadership activities in ways that involve all members of the school community in becoming culturally proficient through having access to a curriculum and instruction program that meets the needs of the entire school community.

The Guiding Principles are the core values held by culturally proficient school leaders and teachers. These core values open up opportunities to build culturally proficient and functionally diverse communities in which people interact with one another in respectful and culturally responsive ways.

Reflection Activity

Take a moment and reread Table 1.3. What thoughts or feelings occur for you? In what ways are the Guiding Principles consistent with how you view yourself as an educator? Given these core values, in what ways might you want to consider your own values differently? How might these guiding principles guide decision-making and policy-setting processes? What might be some implications of one's shift in thinking aligned to the Guiding Principles? Please use the space below to record your responses.

_____

_____

_____

_____

Tool 3: The Continuum—A Perspective for Our Work

Guiding Question: How do we assess ourselves as individuals and as members of our learning community?

Whereas the Guiding Principles of Cultural Proficiency (Table 1.3) provide a frame for personal values and organizational policies, the Cultural Proficiency Continuum provides a guide for the *behaviors* of educators and the *practices* of learning communities and schools. The Continuum displayed in Table 1.4 describes unhealthy and healthy values and behaviors of educators and the policies and practices of schools; in other words, it provides a distinction between what is wrong, unfair, unproductive, and unjust to the left side of the continuum (i.e., destructiveness, incapacity, blindness) and what is right, fair, productive, and just to the right side of the Continuum (i.e., precompetence, competence, proficiency).

Table 1.4 describes the six points of the Continuum. Take a moment to examine the table closely, noting the action words on each side of the Continuum. Behaviors and practices located on the left side of the Continuum (i.e., destructiveness, incapacity, blindness)

Table 1.4   The Cultural Proficiency Continuum: Depicting Unhealthy and Healthy Practices

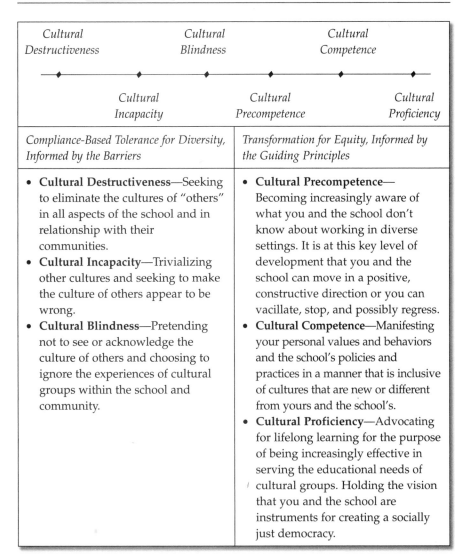

Compliance-Based Tolerance for Diversity, Informed by the Barriers	*Transformation for Equity, Informed by the Guiding Principles*
• **Cultural Destructiveness**—Seeking to eliminate the cultures of "others" in all aspects of the school and in relationship with their communities. • **Cultural Incapacity**—Trivializing other cultures and seeking to make the culture of others appear to be wrong. • **Cultural Blindness**—Pretending not to see or acknowledge the culture of others and choosing to ignore the experiences of cultural groups within the school and community.	• **Cultural Precompetence**—Becoming increasingly aware of what you and the school don't know about working in diverse settings. It is at this key level of development that you and the school can move in a positive, constructive direction or you can vacillate, stop, and possibly regress. • **Cultural Competence**—Manifesting your personal values and behaviors and the school's policies and practices in a manner that is inclusive of cultures that are new or different from yours and the school's. • **Cultural Proficiency**—Advocating for lifelong learning for the purpose of being increasingly effective in serving the educational needs of cultural groups. Holding the vision that you and the school are instruments for creating a socially just democracy.

Source: Adapted from *Culturally Proficient Leadership: The Personal Journey Begins Within,* 2009, by Raymond D. Terrell and Randall B. Lindsey, Thousand Oaks, CA: Corwin.

give evidence of barriers. Behaviors and practices on the right side of the Continuum (i.e., precompetence, competence, proficiency), specifically those regarded as culturally competent and proficient, reflect commitment to the Guiding Principles as educators and schools' doing what is right for our students.

Reflection Activity

Now that you have studied the Continuum, what are your thoughts and reactions? Where do you see yourself relative to the students in your school? What might be some practices within your school community that represent the points along the Continuum? How might you and your colleagues make use of this Continuum as part of your personal and professional learning? Please use the space below to record your responses.

Currently, school-wide efforts to increase cultural competence

Tool 4: Five Essential Elements—The *How* of Our Work

Guiding Question: Do our actions align with who we say we are as a learning community?

Most of us want our educational practices to be situated to the right side of the Continuum but may not know how to get there and may not have the resolve to ask the difficult questions, such as *Why not?* By using the Guiding Principles as an ethical framework and the Continuum to frame our practice, the Essential Elements of Cultural Proficiency serve as standards for educators and schools alike. These five elements become the standards against which we measure the efficacy of our curriculum, the effectiveness of instructional strategies, the relevance of professional development, the utility of systems of assessment and accountability, and the intent of parent and community communications and outreach.

The five Essential Elements provide standards for educators and schools; in other words, they provide for the alignment of ethical principles with educator behaviors and school practices. Table 1.5 contains concise descriptions of the essential elements. Please note

Table 1.5   The Essential Elements for Culturally Proficient Practices

- **Assessing Cultural Knowledge**—Learning about others' cultures, about how educators and the school as a whole react to others' cultures, and what you need to do to be effective in cross-cultural situations. Also, leading for learning about the school and its grade levels and departments as cultural entities.
- **Valuing Diversity**—Creating informal and formal decision-making groups inclusive of people whose viewpoints and experiences are different from yours and the dominant group at the school and that will enrich conversations, decision making, and problem solving.
- **Managing the Dynamics of Difference**—Modeling problem solving and conflict resolution strategies as a natural and normal process within the culture of the schools and the cultural contexts of the communities of your school.
- **Adapting to Diversity**—Learning about cultural groups different from your own and the ability to use others' cultural experiences and backgrounds in all school settings.
- **Institutionalizing Cultural Knowledge**—Making learning about cultural groups and their experiences and perspectives an integral part of the school's professional development.

Source: Adapted from *Culturally Proficient Leadership: The Personal Journey Begins Within*, 2009, by Raymond D. Terrell and Randall B. Lindsey, Thousand Oaks, CA: Corwin.

the empowering language of action that is part of each element. Each element serves as a standard for individual professional behavior and schoolwide practices.

The Essential Elements exist at the *cultural competence* point of the Continuum (Table 1.4). *Cultural Proficiency* is when an educator or school has incorporated the Essential Elements into their practice to the extent that they develop at least these intentional and ongoing commitments:

- A commitment to social justice that addresses the educational needs of all current and emerging cultural groups in the school and community
- A commitment to advocacy that is natural, normal, and effective
- A commitment to mentoring the underserved to have access to educational opportunity and to mentoring those well served by current practice to become aware of and responsive to underserved individuals and cultural groups—the underserved could be colleagues, students, and/or members of the community

REFLECTION

How do you react to the Essential Elements of Cultural Proficiency? In what ways do these elements support your current practices? To what extent do you want these standards to guide your educational practice and that of your school? Please use the space below to record your responses.

_____

_____

_____

_____

GOING DEEPER: 3 KEYS

What are 3 key learnings from this chapter? What are 3 key quotes or comments from the chapter that resonate with you? What are 3 key questions you now have? Thinking of your role as an educator, how does the information from this chapter cause you to think about your practice? In what ways does this information cause you to think differently about your school or district?

We need to work harder to serve those
that are underserved by education

_____

_____

_____

_____

_____

_____

A recurring theme in this book is the importance of *context*. In the same manner that your classroom, school, or community provides a context for your work as an educator, our history provides a context within which we function. Chapter 2 provides important information for you as you understand at ever-deeper levels what it means to provide education to all demographic groups of students in democratic societies that have struggled with equity and diversity.

2

Getting Centered

Our History

The future is in our hands. . . . A history that leaves out minorities reinforces separation, but an inclusive history bridges the divide.

—Takaki, 2008, p. 435

Getting Centered

As you read Takaki's words in the epigraph, what thoughts about North America's histories come to mind? Whose history is told through our textbooks, media, and curricula? When you read or hear terms such as *segregation, integration, equity,* or *diversity,* what images, thoughts, feelings, or reactions occur for you? When these terms are used in your professional settings, what reactions do you observe in your colleagues? Please use the space below to provide responses that describe your and your colleagues' responses.

_____

_____

_____

_____

Being a member of a learning community can be exciting as we learn and apply curricula and instructional strategies that increase the likelihood of our students' academic and social success. In Chapter 1, we described the importance of context for our students, our communities, and ourselves. This chapter provides a brief overview of the history of equity in Canada and the United States as another context for insuring the success of our learning communities. In the same way that culture is important in our society, our histories are important in that they provide great insight into the educational gaps that we are addressing in our schools today.

Equity as a Learning Community Topic

If you are early in your career as an educator, the topic of equity in education is somewhat familiar. Most likely it is an educational topic that is as natural and normal to you as are subjects such as differentiated instruction, professional learning communities, and standards-based assessments. However, if you are an experienced, veteran educator, you have seen these topics emerge during the span of your career. While each of these topics has had its own evolution in our educational practices, the topic of equity has evolved as part of larger national dynamics. For schools especially, dealing with equity issues and topics is a continuing, evolving process.

Whether a new or veteran educator, a question that may arise for you is, *If we are a learning community, then why focus on issues of equity, why not just focus on doing a good job?* This book is devoted to responding to that question, and we begin by tracing some of the important issues involving equity that have unfolded for the last two generations. As your learning community continues to mature and evolve, one of the things you will encounter is that each of your colleagues has a different life story that has influenced their successes and challenges. The more diverse your learning community is, the more varied the life stories are likely to be.

Similar to our life stories, the communities we serve have multiple and varied stories, many of which are filled with instances of segregation and inequity that persist in many communities today. A distinct advantage for our schools, and in particular our learning communities, is our ability to identify the structures within our own values and behaviors and the policies and practices of our schools that either facilitate or inhibit student learning. Having an understanding of our history of equity and inequity is an important step in our learning how to become a culturally proficient learning community.

One of the more frustrating aspects of serving as a professional educator is being confronted in the popular media with pronouncements about the utter failure of public education. Declarations about the failure of public education in the United States were amplified by the report *A Nation at Risk: The Imperative for Educational Reform* (National Commission on Excellence in Education, 1983). Even though the findings of that widely distributed report were called into question by another much less publicized report that was also authorized by the executive branch of the federal government (Wartell & Huelskamp, 1991), myths about the failure of public education have been propounded. Actually, the findings of *A Nation at Risk* weren't as mythical as they were carefully selected.

A significant weakness of *A Nation at Risk* (National Commission on Excellence in Education, 1983) was its rush to label public education as failing rather than report the most important issue, namely the existence of the achievement gap. The cultural and demographic groups of students who had historically done well in our schools were still achieving well; what was new in the widely distributed 1983 report was the increased percentage of students from low socioeconomic and racial or ethnic minority populations who were not as academically successful—their academic test results depressed overall school performance averages. If there is good news from today's accountability mandates, it is that attention is being paid to the achievement gap as an issue that society and schools must serve and that the achievement gap is not seen as an artifact of cultural *differences*. However, the damage was done and the myths about failing public education have continued.

An Equity Context for Schools

This section is designed to provide a historical context for considering equity issues within the formal and informal learning communities in your school. As educators serious about responding to the educational needs of all our students, we believe a description of equity and equality in our schools may serve to better equip you in your professional endeavors.

The histories of Canada and the United States are ones of continuously expanding the opportunities of a democratic society to ever more people. The years since the founding of our democracies have been years of marvelous successes for some of our citizens and years where others struggled for basic freedoms. Some people immigrated to our countries and in two to three generations were able to build independent lives for their families and their communities. However, other people were systematically discriminated against, whether already here or brought to this country forcefully. Even among those who were the objects of intentional discrimination, many have become economically and socially successful, but not in the proportions of those who never faced discrimination.

In the United States, many purport a historic national image of the "rugged individualists" who worked hard against daunting odds in order to become successful. However, that claim has to be measured against a legacy of wars of oppression fought to subjugate First Nations People, a civil war fought in part to free African slaves, and a systematic denial of access to the fruits of democracy due to people's skin color, gender, sexual orientation, faith, ableness, and native language. Since World War II, explicit progress has been made through the use of executive orders, federal and state legislation, and decisions at all levels of the judiciary that seek to counter both active discrimination and systemic, systematic forms of oppression.

The challenge for those of us who lead schools is that both of these very different experiences of success and oppression vie for attention in our schools. Too often, our history and literature courses venerate the former stories and minimize the latter ones. Today, both stories persist in our schools in the form of differential achievement. No matter how one might find fault with the accountability movement, at least it has brought the reality of achievement and educational gaps to the attention of our countries. The sad reality is that those access and achievement gaps are historical, but they have remained invisible to most of the educational community due to our selective vision and our choice to see only the data we want to see.

The integrity of the Cultural Proficiency approach rests on being direct and honest about the historical downside of our societies and on pointing to democratic approaches for healthy responses to inequity. The continuum and essential elements introduced in Chapter 1 and developed more deeply in Chapters 5 through 9 represent democratic approaches to the education of all students. The journey to developing democratic schools, classrooms, teachers, school leaders, and community members has been and is fraught with interruptions and barriers.

As you read the rest of the chapter, think of your current school or classroom and reflect on the extent to which any of these occurrences is present in your students' experiences, their parents' or guardians' experiences, your curriculum, or your colleagues' experiences.

School Segregation

Prior to the 1950s, the separation of students by racial, gender, ethnic, language, and/or national origin groups was based in decisions supported by executive, legislative, and judicial decisions throughout our countries. Illustrations of those actions include:

- Legal forms of segregation in the southern United States that began with slavery and were codified after the Civil War into Jim Crow laws, which defined racial groups and mandated the separation of those races in public settings (e.g., in schools, busses, and restaurants). These practices were based on legislative decisions made by southern states and upheld by state and federal court review.
- Restrictive covenants that have been used throughout Canada and the United States to enforce neighborhood and business patterns.
- The placement of First Nations people on reservations throughout the nineteenth and twentieth centuries. First Nations people, once located to the reservations, were often moved again to less desirable locations when valuable mineral deposits or otherwise desirable property were made available to people of northern European descent.
- Provided impetus by the Mexican Cession of 1848, the encroachment that had been under way for well over a century in what is now the southwestern United States removed native residents from the political, economic, and educational mainstream and increasingly marginalized native residents as European Americans immigrated into that area.
- The Chinese Exclusion Acts of 1882 and 1902 were federal legislative acts supported by the executive and judicial branches of the U.S. government. These acts of Congress were specifically designed to control and minimize immigration once the Chinese were no longer needed for labor-intensive projects such as building railroads throughout the western United States.
- Legally sanctioned segregation in both Canada and the United States resulted in citizens of Japanese ancestry being herded into internment camps during World War II.

Though most of us have some awareness of these phases of our country's histories, and some of us have lived these phases of our histories, it is a legacy that is rarely discussed in educational circles and continues to have influence throughout our social and educational system. These dark periods in our histories created deep and cruel inequities that persist within our nations today. The United States expresses foundational values of liberty and justice for all. The conflict between those foundational values and our everyday behavior and experience is real and painful for many underserved students in our schools. It is not easy to "get over" these dark periods in our history due to the inequities that they created at the time, and it is necessary to acknowledge the sense of inequity that endures today. The events described in this section are testimony to the reality that the equity movement is historical and demands our continued attention as educators.

Desegregation

Desegregation is the legal response in the United States to segregation. Desegregation is just as the term implies, it is to *de-segregate* our society—namely schools for our purpose with this book. There are landmark cases, most of which are well known to readers. We review them here, not only to bring our recent past to our collective attention, but also to let us know that equity has been an arduous struggle. Examples of landmark cases include:

- The 1954 *Brown v. Topeka Board of Education* decisions ended segregation in public facilities and had its genesis in numerous legal initiatives, such as the 1947 California case, *Mendez v. Westminster*, that struck down separate schools for Mexican-American and white students. Both decisions drew their rationales from the equal protection clause of the 14th amendment to the U.S. Constitution.
- Though the *Brown* decisions officially ended *de jure* segregation, *de facto* segregation did not end. To this day, *de facto* segregation— segregation practices that are not the result of legal mandates— continues. Nonetheless, the *Brown* decisions provided the legal and political leverage by which segregation policies and practices in schools could be legally dismantled.

Integration for Equal Access and Equal Rights

The shift from desegregation to integration was of monumental proportions in the history of the United States. Although school desegregation focused initially on the separation of black and white people, in the western and southwestern United States, Latino and

First Nation children were included in the desegregation programs. The 1960s was a period of activism for social justice, with the push for civil rights that included women and other cultural groups. Integration was evidenced in the following ways:

- The Civil Rights Act of 1964 legally ended segregation in all public places; however, the Act was ineffective, as has usually been the case when disenfranchised groups have used the courts and the legislatures to seek redress of their grievances.
- The reality of school desegregation has been beset with problems from the very beginning. Despite many successes in which children benefited from school desegregation (Hawley, 1983; Orfield & Frankenberg, 2007), public attention continued to focus on cases of resistance and failure. Private academies quickly emerged to offer segregated alternatives to European American students, first in the southern United States and later throughout the country. Concurrent with expansion of cities into suburbs in the 1960s was flight to escape unwanted assignments to schools in urban areas. In some cases, these parents did not want to have their children attend a school outside their neighborhood, but in many cases, parents simply wanted to isolate their kids from children with cultural backgrounds different from their own. Too often, white parents viewed children who were racially and ethnically different from themselves as genetically or culturally inferior. Children and parents who were the targets of these reactions often became alienated from the dominant culture.
- The desegregation of schools had two consequences, one intended and the other seemingly unintended. First, voluntary and mandatory school desegregation efforts were designed to provide children of color with the same opportunities white children were receiving. Second, the expansion of entitlement programs (e.g., Title I of the Elementary and Secondary Education Act and the Emergency School Assistance Act) led to many children of color being placed in programs labeled for the culturally and economically *disadvantaged*. Irrespective of the intentionality of the consequence of these programs, the labels became permanently associated with ethnicity, and students in desegregated schools continued to receive substandard education. The labels and practices, created and designed by the dominant culture and paid for by federally funded programs, assisted in maintaining the ineffectiveness of legal desegregation. During

this era, we educators became aware of the effect of teacher expectations, gender bias, and second-language acquisition on the quality of instruction.

- Educators and community supporters engaged in providing special needs students with full access to mainstream educational programs through the due process clause of the 1954 Brown v. Topeka U.S. Supreme Court decision to gain access to public schools in unprecedented ways. Legislation has been crafted and implemented that provides equitable educational opportunities to special needs populations. Principal among federal laws are Public Law 94–142, *Education for All Handicapped Children Act* (1975), Public Law 101–476, *Individuals with Disabilities Act* (1990), and H.R. 1350, *Reauthorization of IDEA* (2004), which is designed to apply the standards-reforms of NCLB to special needs students (Terrell & Lindsey, 2009).

Equal Benefits and Multiculturalism

With the 1970s came new energy for the civil rights movement. The push for equal rights by women and people of color, which has its roots in the very founding of our country, had a focus. The energy spawned by legislative and judicial successes saw women and people of color striving to extend the legal gains won during previous decades to broader societal contexts, including schools. Educators encountering children of diverse cultures in their classrooms, often for the first time, requested new approaches, strategies, and techniques for teaching them. This demand led to the educational emphasis on multicultural-ism, which is a radical departure from the assimilationist, or melting pot, model. It must be noted, though, that the melting pot model had worked well for eastern and southern Europeans but did not work as well for people of color. Concurrently, women's issues emerged to take a prominent place in many schools' professional development activities. Though not prominent in many schools, in the broader society, gay men and lesbians became increasingly vocal in advocating for their rights and access to equal opportunities and benefits.

Diversity

As corporations in Canada and the United States continued to expand into international venues and realize the growing diversity in the labor pools, their executives recognized it was good business to address diversity-related issues. Diversity training for managers and other employees took its place alongside marketing, recruitment, and leadership development. As is often the case, our PK–12 school systems took cues from the business sector, and forward-looking schools and school districts began to seek, create, and implement diversity-related programs ostensibly to support classroom teachers in working with students culturally different from themselves. The upside of many of these programs was the creation of awareness of difference by participants, while the downside is that too often they were disconnected from the daily routines of curriculum and instruction.

Scholars such as James Banks (1994), Ron Edmonds (1979), Geneva Gay (2000), bell hooks (1990), Asa Hilliard (1991), and Myra and David Sadker (1994), among others, connected the business of schooling to diversity issues for those who were interested in reading and learning. Also, during this era, aspects of diversity began to be expanded from ethnicity, language, and gender to include sexual orientation, ableness, and age.

Into the Twenty-First Century: Cultural Competence and Cultural Proficiency

The Essential Elements of Cultural Proficiency provide basic behavior standards for educators to effectively interact with colleagues, students, parents or guardians, and community members who are culturally different from them. Cultural Proficiency is a way of being that enables people to successfully engage in new environments. The works of Comer (1988), Levin (1988), Sizer (1985), Slavin (1990, 1996), Nieto (2004), and Orfield and Frankenberg (2007) are consistent with the basic tenets of Cultural Proficiency. These prominent researchers believe that all children can learn, and their research demonstrates that children from any neighborhood can learn well if they are taught well. Although the national debate over school desegregation has not ended, it now focuses on the equitable distribution of human and capital resources. One of the many contemporary trends in education focuses on finding ways to appreciate the rich differences among students. Many educators wonder how—or even whether—the previous decade's focus on multiculturalism really differs from the next decade's emphasis on diversity.

This shift is not merely a superficial change in terminology but a much-needed, profound change in perspective (Nieto, 2004). Unlike the trend toward multiculturalism, which focused narrowly on students' ethnic and racial differences, the shift toward diversity responds to societal trends by urging us to take a broader approach to addressing equity issues, encompassing a wide range of differences, including race, culture, language, class, caste, ethnicity, gender, sexual orientation, and physical and sensory abilities among students.

Equity and Professional Communities Learning = *Will*

Issues related to equity are not new, no more than is the achievement gap. What has emerged in this generation that commands our attention is the opportunity to make a commitment to provide equitable access to educational opportunity. Prominent scholars, researchers, and social commentators have pressed the issue for equity in our schools for two generations. Edmonds (1979) identified correlates for schools effective for all students, yet we continue to "discover" those factors as new. Hilliard (1991) challenged us and asked if we had the *will* to educate all children. Kozol (1991, 2005, 2007) described what is occurring in too many schools with the terms *shame* and *savage inequalities*. Berliner (2006) made a compelling and chilling case for the profundity of poverty and its effect on our schools, educational policy, and society. Importantly, Berliner (2006) illustrated the intersection of poverty *and* race/ethnicity that undercuts the notion prevalent in some professional development circles that the achievement gap is only a socioeconomic issue.

The opportunity that learning communities possess is the willingness and ability to convene as communities to examine who they are and who they want to be in relationship to the communities they serve. Learning communities, by definition, are intentional in what they learn and what they want to learn. Culturally proficient learning communities place learning within the context of the cultural communities they serve. Knowing the histories of our local school communities as well as knowing our national histories helps us bridge those divides created by exclusion by developing inclusive futures.

REFLECTION

What might be issues of inequity facing your school community? In what ways are resources shared among community members? Who is involved in decision making? Record your responses in the space below:

_____

_____

_____

_____

GOING DEEPER: 3 KEYS

What are 3 key learnings from this chapter? What are 3 key quotes or comments from the chapter that resonate with you? What are 3 key questions you now have? Thinking of your role as an educator, how does the information from this chapter cause you to think about your practice? In what ways does this information cause you to think differently about your school or district?

_____

_____

_____

_____

_____

_____

_____

_____

_____

3

Getting Centered

The Evolution of Learning Communities

We can work to change the embedded structures so that our schools become more hospitable places for student and adult learning. But little will really change unless we change ourselves.

—Barth, 1991, p. 128

Getting Centered

Many educators have told stories of successful schools and the key elements that insured their success. Researchers have found evidence that schools that share a common vision, work collaboratively, share decision making, engage in continuous learning, and experience supportive leadership environments have the potential to increase every student's journey to success (Garmston & Wellman, 2008; Hord & Sommers, 2008; Louis & Kruse, 1995; Dufour & Eaker, 1998).

In what ways do you and your colleagues embrace or question the value and power of learning communities? In your school, what support or resistance exists to move from isolation to collaboration—to working side by side—to inquiring and valuing the contributions and perspectives of your colleagues, your community, your students, and their families? What would it take in your school to have environments that provide the leadership and support to sustain the creativity and vitality of your learning communities? Please use the space below to record your responses to the questions that pique your interest.

_____

_____

_____

_____

Lawrence Lezotte asked, in support of establishing learning communities in our schools, "How much more proof do we need to convince ourselves and our educational systems to do what's right for kids?" (personal communication, June 23, 2004).

Scattered throughout our school systems, teachers are collaborating in learning communities and valuing the contributions and different perspectives each member brings to nourish the academic and social needs of students and their families. However, too often, these learning communities are random and informal rather than formal, structured, and systemic. Many informal learning communities live on the fringes of the work rather than being infused into everyday practice. Often, these groups are formed around their common needs and practices. In his study of groups who came together to improve their ways of working, Wenger (1998) referred to these groups as *communities of practice*. Educators rely on these informal learning communities for day-to-day support, survival, and mentoring.

Given the complexity of schools' structures and cultures, educators look to each other as informal communities of practice to help develop initiatives and interventions in response to student and community needs. Today, some educational communities are more intentional in providing structured time for conversations within formal communities of practice, more commonly known as professional learning communities. These structured conversations provide opportunities for talking about differences in cultures, languages, and student needs. Far too often, people who devalue those who are different negatively impact the momentum and spirit of leaders and learning communities. Such egocentric behaviors tarnish the brilliance of those working for excellence and the success of all students. However, skillful leaders are able to shift the conversations from blaming students and their circumstances to taking professional responsibility for the achievement of all students. These conversations require creating appropriate conditions and building a safety net to have a different type of conversation about staff and administrators' needs and doing something about those needs. The culturally proficient school leader is mindful of engaging the most pessimistic educators in ways that highlight our professional learning and provide opportunities to impact student achievement rather than trying to convince the naysayers to change their minds.

This book is about continually and consciously seeking the best in one another as we work together in a culturally proficient learning community. Focusing on the assets within the educator community rather than focusing on the perceived deficits of our students and their cultures often requires a paradigm shift in people's thoughts and actions—from blaming students and their cultures to asking of ourselves, "What can we learn and do that will enable us to be more successful with our students?"

This chapter highlights the evolution and foundational characteristics of learning communities. We use the lens of Cultural Proficiency to examine learning communities with the intent of strengthening the power and impact of educators who learn together.

A Modern History of Reform

Educational reform has cycled throughout the late nineteenth and twentieth centuries with efforts to improve students' learning (Owens, 1995). Whereas earlier school reform efforts tended to occur, as Owens described, as natural diffusion where "new ideas and practices arose in some fashion and spread in some unplanned way" (p. 209), the modern educational reform is noteworthy in its being led by federal and state governments.

As indicated in Chapter 2, in 1983, the first wave of modern, government-led educational reform emerged in response to *A Nation at Risk* (National Commission on Excellence in Education, 1983). In truth, the jury is still out as to the effects of the modern wave of reform. Evaluations range from "utter failure" (Ravitch, 2003), to "falling short of expectations" (Fuhrman & Elmore, 2004), to "finally uncovering the distasteful truth of disparities in educational success based on student demographics of race, ethnicity, gender, socio-economic status, and ableness" (Bracey, 2006). Irrespective of the varied perspectives on whether or not current reform efforts are having successes, it can't be disputed that the various reform initiatives have definitely informed the conversations among and between educators and the communities we serve. Each of the reform efforts has introduced, and in some cases re-introduced, new language and concepts into our conversations.

The following are concepts and terms from recent and current educational efforts that inform our work about culturally proficient educational practices:

- State adopted curricula and content standards, expanded standardized testing, more strenuous graduation requirements, and stricter standards for teacher certification. *A Nation at Risk* (National Commission on Excellence in Education, 1983) ushered in the national focus on standards for student achievement and teacher performance. While we recognize that there are conflicting views on the effectiveness of what followed *A Nation at Risk*, it is our belief that the document focused attention on historically underserved student groups in unprecedented ways.
- Restructuring and delving more deeply into understanding curricular content. Concern over the lack of student progress led to Goals 2000: Education America Act (1994), which identified specific goals for the U.S. educational system. Goals 2000 gave us the *what* of expected outcomes for students as educators struggled to bring excellence and high achievement to all students in our public schools. Though overly ambitious, Goals 2000 continued to deepen the focus on historically underserved students and opened the door to identifying state-developed content and performance standards for student achievement.
- Assessment and accountability accompanied by rewards and sanctions. The No Child Left Behind Act (NCLB) (2001), the reauthorization of Title I of the Elementary and Secondary Education Act, along with many state-level reforms, such as California's Public School Accountability Act (1999), deepened the conversation and standards-based educational programs and caught the attention of school district superintendents and board members by demanding publicly-reported accountability data for all demographic groups of students. No longer could schools either report schoolwide averages that ignored underserved student populations or shrug off student failure by attributing it to the influence of students' neighborhoods or cultures.

Our charge, at this stage of school reform, is to embrace what Fullan (2003) termed our *moral imperative* and to identify how to serve historically underserved students.

Fullan (2003) stated that everyone, ultimately, has a stake in the caliber of schools; education is everyone's business. As culturally proficient learning communities, our moral imperative is knowing and responding to the cognitive and social needs of all children, with an emphasis on addressing the needs of those who have not been served well in the past. Even with the limitations of NCLB, Lezotte reflected our view as he challenged educators to use a different lens when he said, "NCLB is a required opportunity for educational leaders. Do we want to focus on the required or the opportunity part?" (L. Lezotte, personal communication, June 24, 2004). The assessment processes of NCLB make visible the students who had been invisible. As we disaggregate achievement data we make public the achievement disparities among our various student populations. Although these gaps may be new information to some members of our communities, these national performance gaps have been well documented since 1971 by the National Assessment of Educational Progress (Perie, Moran, & Lutkus, 2005). At minimum, NCLB provides us with the urgency and the opportunity to focus on educating *all* children to attain high levels of achievement.

Cultural Proficiency Intersects With Reform Efforts

The Tools of Cultural Proficiency provide both the moral perspective and ethical framework for delving within ourselves as educators and inquiring within our schools' policies and practices to learn how to better serve culturally diverse student populations. In learning new ways of serving our communities, we reculture our schools. Old practices that sought to blame the students, their parents or guardians, their impoverished neighborhoods, or their cultures for underperformance are replaced by practices that recognize that students are being underserved and are grounded in appropriate curricula, differentiated instruction, and relevant assessment strategies. Educators who make the paradigmatic shift to being responsible for better serving their students are engaged as culturally proficient learning communities.

Shifting From Compliance to Transformation

Educators working together is not new information. As previously indicated, educational reform is hardly new. Waves of educational reform have coursed through schools since the late nineteenth century (Owens, 1995). What is new today is the inclusion of historically underserved students in unprecedented ways. That is to say, we are now expected and required to educate all children to high levels, inclusive of their cultural or demographic memberships. The Tools for Cultural Proficiency help transform school leaders' thinking from accountability as a matter of compliance to thinking about accountability as their moral, professional responsibility.

Learning Communities Evolve in Response to Reform Efforts

A distinctive feature of current reform efforts has been the emergence of the term *learning communities*. Berman and others (Berman, McLaughlin, Bass-Golod, Pauly, & Zellman, 1977) noted that teachers were working together to shape their own learning and professional development, which is critical to sustaining innovations and change in educational systems. Three decades of research and expert testimony strongly support the power of learning communities in generating professional learning (Senge, 1990; McLaughlin, 1990; Sergiovanni, 1991; Louis & Kruse, 1995; Hord, 1992; and DuFour & Eaker, 1998). With this book, we add to this body of knowledge by using the lens of Cultural Proficiency to examine how learning communities can transform their cultures into being more inclusive and valuing diversity.

As a parent, guardian, aunt, uncle, or grandparent, we all want our children to be in the class with that educator who fills them with excitement and infectious enthusiasm for learning, inquiry, and discovery—no matter the ethnicity, family, religion, gender, sexual orientation, or socioeconomic status of the educator or student. We all want our children to be in the class with the educator who learns with and from our children, while our children learn from each other. Professionals who come together with a common desire to learn in community, to inquire into expanded possibilities, and to strive for continually improving professional practices are recognized through terminology such as

- communities of practice (Wenger, 1998; Wenger, McDermott, & Snyder, 2002),
- learning organizations (Senge, 1990),
- learning communities (Sergiovanni, 1991),

- school-based professional community, (Louis & Kruse, 1995),
- professional learning communities (Hord, 1997; DuFour & Eaker, 1998), and
- small learning communities (Raywid, 1996; Cotton, 1996; Oxley, 2001).

The Etymology of Learning Communities

In response to the challenge to meet the needs of all our children, successful schools of the twenty-first century are moving beyond reform and restructure to engaging in the process of reculturing schools in order to become learning communities. Senge (1990) defined a learning organization as "one in which people are continually learning how to learn together" (p. x). In their highly original and influential book, *Schools That Learn: A Fifth Discipline Fieldbook for Educators, Parents, and Everyone Who Cares About Education*, Senge et al. (2000) reflected on school reform:

> The idea of a school that can learn has become increasingly prominent during the last few years. It is becoming clear that schools can be re-created, made vital, and sustainably renewed not by fiat or command, and not by regulation, but by taking a learning orientation. This means involving everyone in the system in expressing their aspirations, building their awareness, and developing their capabilities together. (p. 5)

As we considered the various constructs of learning communities, we designed Table 3.1 to identify the elements of Senge (1990), Wenger (1998), Louis and Kruse (1995), DuFour and Eaker (1998), and Oxley (2001) in relation to Shirley Hord's (1997) five tenets of professional learning communities. In conducting our study for the most efficient manner to fuse Cultural Proficiency with learning communities, we arrived at Hord's tenets being most useful for our purposes. However, given the prominence and influence of the work of Senge, Wenger, Louis and Kruse, DuFour and Eaker, and Oxley, a review of their major elements is presented in Table 3.1.

The following paragraphs provide brief summaries of the major researchers' work. We provide these summaries in response to the oft-asked question, "So, where did the term *learning community* and its various derivations, such as *professional learning communities* and *small learning communities,* originate?"

Table 3.1 Evolution of Learning Communities

Shirley Hord	Peter Senge	Etienne Wenger	Karen Seashore Louis and Sharon Kruse	Richard DuFour and Robert Eaker	Diana Oxley
Professional Learning Communities	*Learning Organizations/Communities of Commitment*	*Communities of Practice*	*School-Based Learning*	*Professional Learning Communities*	*Small Learning Communities (SLC) Within Secondary Reform*
Shared values and vision	Shared vision; shared mental models	Learning provided strategic relevance for the organization; participants shared a common purpose and passion	Shared norms and values; shared sense of responsibility for all students	Shared mission, vision, values, goals	Shared vision for small, personalized environments with academic rigor and high achievement for all students
Supportive and shared leadership	Systems thinking	Voluntary core participants provided shared leadership	Shared sense of responsibility for all students		Inclusive program and practices; autonomous/semi-autonomous SLCs with shared leadership
Collective learning and application	Team learning	Voluntary participation of core and active members; contributions from inside and outside perspectives	Move from isolation to collaboration, de-privatization of practice; collaborative focus on student learning	Focus on student learning; continuous improvement	Learning team focus on rigorous, relevant curriculum and instruction; continuous improvement
Supportive organizational conditions	Systems thinking; interconnecting	General lack of formal organizational support	Identified requirements for organizational support		School and district support
Shared personal practice	Personal mastery; team learning	Participation brought personal meaning	Reflective dialogue among teachers	Collaboration	Interdisciplinary teaching and learning teams

Senge's Five Disciplines

Senge's (1990) five disciplines "offer genuine help for dealing with the dilemmas and pressures of education today" (p. 7). The five disciplines include personal mastery, shared vision, mental models, team learning, and systems thinking.

Personal mastery is the practice of comparing one's reality to a clearly articulated personal vision, creating tension that causes one to move closer to realizing that vision. An old Japanese proverb states, "Vision without action is a daydream. Action without vision is a nightmare" (Kotelnikov, 2005).

Shared vision within the organization promotes commitment. Learning communities that cannot commit to action do not realize the vision.

Mental models are a discipline of reflection and inquiry, developing awareness of attitudes and perceptions not only of one's own, but also of those around you. This attention to diversity and the value others bring to the table is critical in a culturally proficient learning community.

Team learning embraces working collaboratively toward common goals. Culturally proficient learning communities can lead to powerful and inclusive collaborative teams in which all voices are sought after, listened to, and valued.

Systems thinking and inclusion allow for understanding the interdependency of our actions.

Applying the lens of Cultural Proficiency to the five disciplines within an educational system focuses on learning that "represents an approach that galvanizes hope" (Senge et al., 2000, p. 10) for significant change and success for all students.

Wenger's Communities of Practice

Wenger (1998) and Wenger, McDermott, & Snyder (2002) described communities of practice as formal and informal groups coming together to share concerns, problems, and passion for a focused topic or area of expertise. Wenger's communities of practice provided personal meaning for the individual and strategic relevance for the organization, moving each toward deep learning, change, innovation, and excellence. Yet "many intentional communities fall apart soon after their initial launch because they don't have enough energy to sustain themselves. Communities, unlike teams and other structures, need to invite the interaction that makes them alive" (Wenger et al., 2002, p. 50).

Louis and Kruse's School-Based Learning

Karen Seashore Louis and Sharon Kruse (1995) described school-based learning, in which educators moved from their traditional position of isolation to one of collaboration, deprivatization of practice, reflective dialogue among teachers, and a collaborative focus on student learning based on shared norms and values. Their 1995 publication identified social and human resources that support professional learning communities. The resources they identified included (a) openness to improvement within an environment that supports risk taking, (b) trust and respect, (c) a cognitive and skill base that reflects effective teaching, (d) supportive instructional leadership, and (e) a focus on socialization in which the vision of professional learning is imparted to new teachers.

Hord's Professional Learning Communities

Shirley Hord coined the phrase professional learning community in 1997. Hord's tenets for a professional learning community include (a) shared values and vision, (b) supportive and shared leadership, (c) collective learning and application, (d) shared personal practice, and (e) supportive organizational conditions, which together result in powerful learning. These tenets are explored in greater detail and are aligned with the Essential Elements of Cultural Proficiency in Chapters 5 through 9 in this book.

DuFour and Eaker's PLCs

In 1998, DuFour and Eaker framed their work at Stevenson High School in Illinois as a professional learning community and identified the key elements as (a) shared mission, vision, values, and goals; (b) collaboration; (c) focus on results; and (d) continuous improvement. Smylie (1995) asserted that, "We will fail, as we have failed so many times before, to improve schooling for children until we acknowledge the importance of schools not only as places for teachers to work but also as places for teachers to learn" (p. 92). Eaker (2004) held that one of the most fundamental differences between schools that function as professional learning communities and their more traditional counterparts is a shift from a focus on teaching to a focus on learning. "Professional learning communities make learning their primary focus" (p. 225).

Oxley's Small Learning Communities

Another type of learning community to emerge in the late 1990s was the small learning community (SLC). Small learning communities are being tried in large, comprehensive high schools; the schools are reorganized into smaller autonomous or semiautonomous units that focus on adult and student relationships as well as learning for both the student and the educator. Small learning communities engage multiple stakeholders from education, families, and community in collaborative learning groups. A common element of the vision of small learning communities is each child succeeding in a rigorous and relevant curriculum supported by a personalized and nurturing culture where the student feels a strong connection to an adult advocate who knows their personal goals, learning styles, and academic and social needs.

Oxley (2001), in a review of the research on small learning communities, stated:

> The term [small learning communities] applied to the practice of organizing high schools into smaller units has undergone many changes over the last four decades. Houses and schools-within-schools came on the scene beginning in the 1960s; magnet programs, career academies, and mini-schools in the 1970s; charters in the late 1980s and 1990s; and finally small learning communities today. The evolution in terms is significant. It parallels development in our thinking about the crucial ingredients of effective education. The earlier terms emphasized small structure and curricular specialization and choice, both crucial to improved teaching, yet not the complete story. Small learning community, in contrast, encompasses these elements and more: a focus on the learner and learning, and in particular, the active and collaborative nature of teachers' and students' works. (p. 1)

Culturally proficient school leaders incorporate the small community aspect of SLCs by structuring schedules for groups of students and teachers to engage in knowing each other and valuing the diversity of each community member as well as the diversity of the group itself. For example, block schedules (60 to 90 minutes per content area), interdisciplinary teams, houses or villages, and student advisory or homeroom periods (15 to 20 minutes) provide middle and high school teachers, counselors, and administrators time to get to know their students in ways that assess and value their students' cultures and their own cultures. These intentionally designed structures support adults' interaction with those who are different and model appropriate behaviors for the students.

Hord's Five Tenets Integrated With Cultural Proficiency

A common denominator among the various elements of learning communities is that schools function as a system in order to be impacted in positive, productive ways. In working with PK–12 educators and college and university faculty who prepare educators for our PK–12 schools, we have recognized the need to have these five elements from Hord and Sommers' (2008) relevant literature in place for all schools and all students:

- Shared beliefs, values, and vision
- Shared and supportive leadership
- Collective learning and its application
- Supportive conditions
- Shared personal practice

We believe the sustainability of learning communities requires reflection on a personal and organizational level. Reflective practice as part of a systems thinking approach is found in Hord and Sommers' (2008) five tenets for a professional learning community. We view their work through the lens of Cultural Proficiency whereby participants in the learning community engage in examining

- their own personal beliefs and values,
- the policies and practices of the school or district,
- the culture of one's community, and
- disaggregated data to create an instructional plan focused on improving achievement of all demographic groups.

In this book, we have rearranged the well known acronym *PLC* to be *PCL*, *Professional Communities, Learning* in order to elevate culture to a level of importance that permits a thorough examination of organizational culture on par with racial, ethnic, gender, social class, sexual orientation, faith, ableness, and language acquisition cultures that abide in our schools. The definition of each word within professional learning communities gives insight into the essence of the three terms within the single concept of professional learning communities:

- *Professional* communicates a sense of excellence and current understanding of best practices. This implies personal mastery, continual learning, and membership within an explicit field of practice.
- *Learning* implies an ongoing curiosity, inquiry, analysis, and continuous improvement—in essence a lifelong learner whose self-directed curiosity leads to intentionally structuring inquiry, asking breakthrough questions, and learning individually as well as in community.
- *Community* conveys a meaning of people working together in positive relationships anchored in trust, effective communication, and a high value of differences.

All three words support the underlying assumption of a professional community, learning—that we can make a difference in student learning.

Our literature review has led us to select Hord and Sommers' (2008) five tenets of a professional learning community as a compatible frame for representing the work of Cultural Proficiency. Following are descriptions of the five tenets in relation to Cultural Proficiency.

Shared Beliefs, Values, and Vision

Generally speaking, individuals act in ways consistent with our deeply held values and beliefs. When teachers, administrators, counselors, and other school community members express these values and beliefs, a common vision and clearly stated mission are more likely to become a reality for the community. Being clear and intentional about our values for student achievement and our beliefs that all children can and do learn are key factors for determining our mission and goals for student success. Judith Bardwick, (1996) in her book, *In Praise of Good Business*, stated that the most important question in any organization has to be "What is the business of our business?" (p. 34). The "business"—or focus—for schools must be learning. The vision of the culturally proficient professional learning community paints the picture of the absolute reality that all demographic communities not only aspire to succeed, they experience and achieve such success. Without the latter, the professional learning community is not culturally proficient.

The culturally proficient vision articulates the behaviors in which all community members will engage and not engage, which align with the "unhealthy and healthy language of the continuum" described in Chapter 1. An inclusive vision guides the policies and practices of the learning community members. Continual communication and assessment of this vision are the keys to the success of the professional learning community members and its leaders.

Shared and Supportive Leadership

Culturally proficient learning communities do not just happen as part of the routine business of schools. As a matter of structure and organization, schools do not naturally support collaboration or community learning. As stated earlier, learning communities are intentional and must be supported, nurtured, and lead by principals and other school and community leaders. Hord and Sommers (2008) stated that "one of the defining characteristics of PLCs is that power, authority, and decision making are shared and encouraged" (p. 11). The traditional culture and structure within our educational system presents barriers to shared leadership. The principal, having authoritative power, may find it difficult to transform her identity from an authoritative figure to one of co-learner, instructional leader, and contributor to the learning community. With community leadership comes responsibility. Teachers, counselors, students, and community members may have concerns and learning needs with this new sense of responsibility. Providing professional development and support leading to successful learning communities has explicit implications for school leaders (Hord & Sommers, 2008). With shared leadership comes the shared responsibility for the learning and success of all students and staff. Aspiring to be culturally proficient school administrators and seeking to broaden the school's leadership, paying attention to equity and the future cultural needs of the school may be achieved by embracing the Guiding Principles and Essential Elements of Cultural Proficiency.

Collective Learning and Its Application

As the term professional learning community implies, staff from all grade levels and departments convene to study collegially and work collaboratively. Educators, students, and community members continuously learn together and apply what they have learned to their work. Applying what they have learned to their work is critical to the work of learning communities, as is inquiry into the impact of that work on moving the organization forward toward the collective vision (Hord & Sommers, 2008). In a culturally proficient learning community, learning goes beyond the protocols of number and data crunching that many professional learning communities do in their time together. Culturally proficient learning communities continually seek to learn and understand the members of their educational community and the students, families, and neighborhoods they serve. Engaging the perspectives and voices of families, students, and the community is critical to the learning of the PLC.

Supportive Conditions

The work of McLaughlin (1990) in the RAND study of innovation and change revealed that once schools adopted an innovation, attention to implementation and support waned over time. Hord and Sommers (2008) identified *supportive conditions* as one of the five elements for establishing and sustaining professional learning communities. She described two categories for support of learning communities:

- Logistics for implementation—the when, where, what, and how the staff regularly and frequently come together as one group to do the reflection, inquiry and learning, problem solving, and decision making of the PLC
- Relationships and human capacity

The major challenges of learning communities are building trust, having high expectations for all members, and meeting the concerns and learning needs of individual members. Cultural Proficiency provides the lens and new way of being—a new identity—to guide and nourish these relationships. Culturally proficient learning communities attend to necessary logistics that value all community members (orientation to time and space, as well as access to materials and resources). For example, culturally proficient community leaders arrange flexible meeting times to insure parents and other community members can attend sessions; resources that reflect all cultural groups and community members with special learning or language needs are provided for community members.

Shared Personal Practice

Hord (1997) and Hord and Sommers (2008) completed the circle of key elements by identifying shared personal practice as the last element of professional learning communities. For all students to experience instruction and curriculum that excites and motivates them to learn demands teachers who share their best practices with colleagues. Yet exposing one's professional practice is often a frightening experience. A culture of trust and respect among and between all members becomes a key element for professional learning communities. It's easy to get some staff members to work well together, to bring together diverse thinking and skills that result in a synergy that becomes the model community. Given that implementing professional learning communities system-wide includes all staff, challenges can emerge when those whose values for human diversity and those who are different rear an ugly face. The traditional isolation of the teacher in the classroom, where individuals "teach science" or "teach math" or other subjects of their passion rather than "teaching students," creates resistance to collaboration. School leaders who intentionally structure conversations and dialogues to help surface these deeply held assumptions, values, and beliefs are aware that these are the initial steps in creating a common, shared vision and mission as a learning community. These leadership actions are not easy, but they are necessary in order to keep the focus on improved student learning.

For example, the principal and leadership team can use the Continuum for Cultural Proficiency (Chapter 1) to create the conversation about how community members talk about and describe their students and their families and languages. The leadership team can use the Essential Elements of Cultural Proficiency as a rubric to assess and develop individual and content-area instructional practices. Culturally proficient action-research projects can be designed by teacher leaders in response to disaggregating data by demographic groups.

As members of the learning community embrace an identity as a culturally proficient learning community, seeing the value others within the educational community bring to the table leads to an abundant banquet of talent and perspectives that can enrich the experiences of all. The mindset to examine assets and possibilities rather than deficits can motivate and sustain those who have the power to lift up our children to great accomplishments and powerful learning.

Culturally Proficient Learning Communities

With the accountability mandated by the No Child Left Behind Act (2001) and our moral imperative to ensure the success of all students and staff, today's educational reform movement focuses with intentionality on creating and sustaining professional learning throughout the system, moving from voluntary and sporadic learning communities to required participation by all staff. With this systemization of learning communities emerge resistance, conflict, and various levels of effectiveness. There are those who say, "This too shall pass." Given the history of the various terminologies used to describe professional learning, it is most likely that new language will be identified to describe those who learn together, as well as new elements added to refine and strengthen the power of professional learning.

While the conversations and implementations of learning communities are on the rise, we notice in each of the learning-community constructs the absence of an explicit framework for Cultural Proficiency. We offer culturally proficient professional communities, learning as a way to provide success for more students than ever before.

So a question we might ask ourselves is, "In what ways do learning communities systematically assess their culture, exhibit the value of the diversity within their community, manage the dynamics of difference found within the community, adapt to those differences, and institutionalize new cultural knowledge?"

REFLECTION

What is your understanding, thus far, of culturally proficient learning communities? In what ways are you and your colleagues in community learning? How might a culturally proficient learning community support your current practices? In what ways might the lens of Cultural Proficiency support your current learning community? Please use the space below to record your responses.

_____

_____

_____

_____

Chapters 5 through 9 are devoted to applying the lens of Cultural Proficiency to Hord and Sommers' (2008) tenets of professional learning communities through the characters in Maple View School District. You will have the opportunity to examine your personal practice and to engage with colleagues in collaborative curiosity and learning.

GOING DEEPER: 3 KEYS

A lot of important information about learning communities was summarized in this chapter. Take a moment and think about your professional perspective as a teacher, an instructional aide, an administrator, a support staff member, a parent or guardian, a student at the school, or a community member. What are 3 key learnings from this chapter? What are 3 key quotes or comments that you take away from this chapter? What 3 key questions are on your mind? What insights or "Aha!" moments about your own professional practice have emerged for you? What observations or questions do you have about your colleagues, grade levels, departments, school, students, or community? Please use the space below to record your responses.

_____

_____

_____

_____

_____

_____

_____

_____

_____

PART II

Voices From the Field

In the Preface, we cautioned you to prepare to be disturbed through curiosity and community. In Chapters 1 through 3, we presented the descriptions and usefulness of the Tools for Cultural Proficiency, the history of equity in schools, and a brief review of professional learning communities. Part II: Voices From the Field establishes Maple View School District and the community it serves as the context for sustaining culturally proficient learning communities. Maple View School District (MVSD) is a pseudonym for the composite of authentic experiences and data collected by the authors. Maple View's voices reflect real stories of communities learning about themselves. Chapter 4 connects a need for professional learning with a goal for culturally proficient practices in the Maple View School District. The Maple View District represents a composite of actual individuals and groups from schools, classrooms, and districts across the U.S. and Canada who are actively engaged in developing culturally proficient learning communities. We use these vignettes to make practical application of the two concepts of Cultural Proficiency and professional learning communities.

The educational leaders of Maple View have been engaged in this journey toward equity for several years. They have actively embraced tools and techniques to assess their organizational cultural as well as individual assessments about cross-cultural interactions. The former and current superintendents have marshaled resources for professional learning and have made public their commitment toward successfully serving all students. Recently, the district and school site leaders intentionally called upon all educators in the district to expand their learning communities (LCs) to more formally engage students, their families, and community members. Learning community leaders (LCLs) attended conferences and received training in formal learning community designs and purposes. For the past school year, LCs have been committed to creating experiences that support high performance learning and confront issues of inequity in the school district.

Chapters 4 through 9 take you behind the scenes of Maple View School District's LCs. You will hear their conversations as they examine data, plan meetings, surface assumptions, struggle with best practices, and confront inequities through collaborative curiosity. Their curiosity becomes focused inquiry about how students in their community are being served. In their newly formed LCs, the educators are using new tools and skills. They are learning to ask new, breakthrough questions to help shift their thinking to curiosity rather than certainty. Together, the teachers, administrators, counselors, school staff, and community business partners are becoming a culturally proficient community focused on learning.

And now a word of caution: Be careful what we ask for. Without appropriate, collaborative, and true leadership focused on collective learning and measurable results, PLCs can become no more than a vehicle for compliance through a progression of steps and checklists. In contrast, culturally proficient learning communities are willing to dig deeper, ask difficult questions, and explore their own assumptions and actions in ways that benefit the students and families they serve. The attributes of professional learning communities and the Essential Elements of Cultural Proficiency do not exist in isolation. These Elements integrate as a whole process for changing the conversations about our students and their families. However, for the purpose of illustrating the practical nature of the concepts (learning communities and Cultural Proficiency), we align each of the characteristics of Hord and Sommers' (2008) descriptions of learning communities with one of the Essential Elements of Cultural Proficiency within the Maple View context. The integration of these components is illustrated in the vignettes in Chapters 4 through 9.

4

Maple View

Sustaining a Culturally Proficient Learning Community

. . . contrary to myth, effective collaborative cultures are not based on like-minded consensus. They value diversity because that is how they get different perspectives and access to ideas to address complex problems. Under such conditions, inequity is far less likely to go unnoticed or to be tolerated.

—Fullan, 1999, p. 37

Getting Centered

Think about Michael Fullan's (1999) quote in the context of the learning communities in which you currently serve or opportunities you have to shape a learning community. What are the strengths and assets of your community? What contributions do you make to the learning of the community? In what ways do you, as a community, collaboratively learn about your students? How do you learn about the families of your students? How do you learn about yourselves, individually and collectively?

Please use the space below to record your responses to the questions that resonate for you.

_____

_____

_____

_____

Maple View, a Professional Community Learning About Itself

This chapter introduces you to the community of Maple View and the Maple View School District (MVSD). Maple View serves as the context for illustrations of developing and sustaining a culturally proficient learning community. The members of the MVSD have been on a school improvement journey for the past six years. Like many school districts across the United States, MVSD teachers, administrators, parents, students, and other community members have been seeking ways to improve student performance as measured by multiple assessment strategies including standardized and performance-based assessments. The district administrators have focused on goals to

- develop a standards-based instructional plan for each school in the district,
- use Cultural Proficiency as an approach for teachers and administrators to become aware of how their own values and beliefs impact and influence the students in their classrooms, and
- use Cultural Proficiency as an approach for teachers and administrators to examine district and school policies and practices that influence, impact, honor, or deny students opportunities to learn and achieve.

This professional journey has been intentional and focused on all students being well served in all areas of the community—irrespective of the race, ethnicity, ableness, gender, sexual orientation, faith, class, or socioeconomic level of the students and their families. The educators of MVSD are dedicated to making each school a high performing school so that all students have opportunities to learn and achieve at levels higher than ever before. For some Maple View students, this dream is becoming reality partly because of the combined efforts of community members, parents, teachers, administrators, and community business partners to become more aware of the student needs aligned with the standards-based instructional system. However, the district is far from reaching its vision and goals for all students. The question facing district and school leaders is, How do we maintain the momentum that we have developed toward standards-based instruction by using the Tools for Cultural Proficiency to support our educators and our community?

Maple View Community

Maple View is a suburban community located within a major metropolitan area. The city's population of 200,000 is composed of mostly low to middle income and working-class folks who live and work within the community. About 5% of Maple View residents are in the upper tax bracket and work in the top-paying management positions in the area's high-tech industries and corporations. About 30% of Maple View residents are considered working poor and rely on government assistance for child care and health care for their families. For the most part, families in this community, regardless of income, send their children to the local public schools, shop at the area businesses, bank at the local banks and credit unions, seek health care at the community hospital and neighborhood clinics, and attend local churches, temples, and synagogues.

Area builders and leading real estate business owners perceive Maple View as a prosperous community partly because of the community's master plan for development. However, the waiting list for low-rent public housing indicates a highly diverse economic environment. A major state highway divides the master-planned, affluent West Side from the downtown and middle- and low-income housing developments of the East Side. A large shopping mall opened five years ago to serve the upscale master-planned community. Mom-and-pop merchants, including a locally owned hardware store and a drugstore owned by the same family for three generations, serve the downtown area on the East Side. The East Side residents typically shop at the downtown stores as well as the nearby big box stores (e.g., Wal-Mart, Target, K-Mart, and Sears). Given the recent downturn in the economy, local financial institutions are beginning to post foreclosure signs in many of the East Side neighborhoods. Local shop owners are facing cutbacks and possible bankruptcy.

Maple View School District

The ethnic diversity of the city's population is reflected in the student population in the local school district. Of the 25,000 public school students, 35% are European Americans; 30% are Latino from Central America, South America, and the Caribbean; 20% are Asian Americans (first- and second-generation families from Korea and the Philippines, and third- and fourth-generation families from China); 10% are African Americans; 3% are Native Americans; and 2% are Pacific Islanders. Twenty percent of the total student population is in special education programs, and 15% of the students are learning English as a second language. The district reports that its students speak 10 different primary languages.

The local school district responded to the increased student population in the West Side area by building the new Pine Hills Elementary School for grades K through 5 and the new Pine View Middle School for students in grades 6 through 8. Three years ago, the district opened the new state-of-the-art Pine Hills High School on the west side of the city to serve all high school students in the district. The old Maple View High School facility on the east side of the city was converted into a community school for at-risk students, adult school students, and community recreation organizations. The school district maintains ownership of the property and has a joint-use partnership agreement with the city council. The downtown and East Side students continue to be served by the original Maple View Elementary School for grades preK through 5 and Maple View Middle School for grades 6 through 8 in the district (Nuri Robins, Lindsey, Lindsey, & Terrell, 2006).

Twin Goals: Culturally Proficient Learning Community to Insure Standards-Based Instruction and Leadership

Dr. Barbara Campbell, the recently retired superintendent of MVSD, serves as an educational consultant to the district. In her former role as MVSD's superintendent, she focused her leadership efforts on creating culturally proficient schools, faculty members, and school leaders. Dr. Campbell and her leadership team spent time working with the county office of education staff, who helped provide resources to establish relationships with numerous local businesses and universities to provide internships and partnerships for the students. Dr. Campbell guided district leaders and teachers in developing a standards-based educational environment for all students. She was aware that although standards had been developed as the district educational plan, many classroom teachers struggled with how to implement standards-based lessons and monitor student progress. School site administrators were unclear about how to monitor teachers' implementation plans.

Dr. Campbell was instrumental in guiding instructional leadership teams composed of site administrators, key teacher leaders, and district office curriculum coordinators to review student achievement data and question why so many students from the east side were not achieving at higher levels. She saw the need to strengthen the connection between teaching to standards and culturally proficient instruction. She was aware that staff development programs often did not go beyond the theory and demonstration level. Dr. Campbell wanted to insure standards-based instruction and assessment skills were applied in all classrooms in the district. The instructional leadership team, with her guidance, selected coaching for Cultural Proficiency as a way to support the implementation of culturally proficient instructional strategies. As superintendent, Dr. Campbell called on Sam Brewer, a colleague who knew and understood the need for the twin goals of the district, to serve as her coach and help her develop a leadership plan for the district.

Sam Brewer, a former teacher and site administrator in the district, was the assistant superintendent of Curriculum, Instruction, and Assessment. Sam has also been on a personal journey to become a culturally proficient educational leader. He recently read an article about the East Side/West Side phenomena in many suburban school districts (Buenida, Ares, Juarez, & Peercy, 2004) and immediately related the author's description with the circumstances in Maple View. Sam was determined to address the issues of inequity that have been influenced by the social, political, cultural, and economic issues of Maple View. Cultural Proficiency is one approach that is helping Sam manage the dynamics of diversity in the school community.

Over the past summer, Sam and a team of teachers and administrators participated in a coaching workshop series called "Developing Culturally Proficient Learning Communities to Improve Student Achievement." Sam and the team members were subsequently asked to serve as instructional coaches to teachers and administrators. He recalls how excited he was when Barbara, then superintendent, called and asked him to serve as her leadership coach. For the past several years, Sam and Barbara have worked together to encourage and support district educators to become more aware of the changing demographics of the community and to view diversity as an opportunity and positive experience rather than a challenge and negative experience. Sam is on his own Cultural Proficiency journey and enjoys conversations with Barbara about his growth. She asked him to use his coaching skills and help her develop a new plan of action to realize the district's vision of all students in the Maple View School District being well served.

As Dr. Campbell planned her retirement from the district, the action plan continued to serve the district toward their vision. In their efforts to sustain the leadership momentum established by Dr. Campbell's leadership team, the Maple View school board recently appointed Sam Brewer the new superintendent. As the school year opened, Sam asked himself, What will it take for us to grow as a culturally proficient learning community?

The Context for Culturally Proficient Learning Communities

Maple View School District sets the context for culturally proficient learning communities throughout this book. The conversations among characters in the vignettes are actual examples of conversations that teachers, counselors, parents, students, and administrators have shared with us as we worked in schools and related organizations. The Maple View story is a composite of data collected from schools and community educators using the Tools of Cultural Proficiency. The MVSD characters appear in Chapters 5 through 9 to illustrate the opportunities to use the five Essential Elements of Cultural Proficiency as standards of behavior for learning communities. We use the Maple View School District to demonstrate how schools in today's assessment-driven environments struggle to make the shift from the traditional subject-focused instructional model to the student-centered, collaborative, standards-based model. This model requires a shift from the language of blaming the students and their circumstances to the language of personal responsibility for teaching and learning (Kegan & Lahey, 2001). Table 4.1 illustrates the language reflected in behaviors and ideas that hold educators trapped in the traditional model of quick fixes and rule making. Examine the shift in language that occurs when community leaders focus on student learning rather than totally on student circumstances. Now read the reflective prompts below and think about your own thinking and reaction to the language shift described in the table.

Table 4.1   Shift to Language of Professional Communities, Learning

Traditional Model for School Improvement From the Language of	Collaborative Model for School Improvement To the Language of
• Compliance • Blame • Immediate solutions and quick fixes • Assumptions that hold us • Rigid rules and policies • Constructive criticism based on judgment and evaluation • Superficial praise of few	• Commitment • Personal and professional responsibility • Collaborative commitments • Assumptions that we hold • Ongoing trust in people and processes • Deconstruction of behaviors and results based on data and inquiry • Public agreement and celebration

Source: Adapted from *How the Way We Talk Can Change the Way We Work: Seven Languages for Transformation,* by Robert Kegan and Lisa Laskow Lahey, 2001, San Francisco: Jossey-Bass.

REFLECTION

Using Table 4.1 as a lens to view your school, what language do you hear at your school? In what ways do stereotypes, assumptions, blame, and negative presuppositions influence the decisions and behaviors of both you and your colleagues? In what ways might you apply your collective learning to demonstrate your value for diversity? Are families perceived as members of the professional learning community and partners in their children's education or as outsiders and disconnected from the learning community?

Please use the space below to record your responses.

_____

_____

_____

_____

GOING DEEPER: 3 KEYS

What are 3 key learnings from this chapter? What are 3 key quotes or comments from the chapter that resonate with you? What are 3 key questions you now have? Thinking of your role as an educator, how does the information from this chapter cause you to think about your practice? What thoughts come to mind about your own context as you read about Maple View?

_____

_____

_____

_____

_____

_____

_____

_____

_____

5

Assessing Cultural Knowledge Through Shared Personal Practice

We can create the most effective generation of leaders ever by redefining and simplifying leadership around the core concepts of professional learning communities. But no one can lead in an environment where differences in practice and learning outcomes are ignored or trivialized. No on can lead where constructive criticism feedback is regarded as an invasion of privacy, an affront to professionalism.

—Schmoker, 2006, p. 29

Getting Centered

The era of accountability that has slowly dawned over public education in this past generation has provided both challenges and opportunities. On the challenging side of the equation, as described in Chapters 1 and 4, the accountability movement has disturbed the system in many ways and has caused fierce resistance that has, in itself, become the focus of too many schools. The consequence of such fierce resistance is a continuing nonattention to disparities in student achievement and success.

The redeeming side of the equation is that many schools are experiencing success in educating students in ways they would not have envisioned a generation ago. Schools that have embraced accountability as opportunity are examining their own practices and modifying them in ways that focus on the academic and social successes of all the cultural groups of their students. A hallmark of these schools is that they embrace accountability as a means to better serve all students.

Given the two scenarios of fierce resistance and accountability for equity, how do you describe the culture of your school with respect to accountability? How do you describe your attitude and behavior regarding educator accountability? As you reread Schmoker's (2006) quote, what comes to mind in relation to professionalism at your school? How are professional success and challenges shared among teachers, administrators, and other community members?

Please use the space below to record your responses to the questions that resonate for you.

_____

_____

_____

_____

Going Deeper With Cultural Proficiency

This chapter is devoted to describing the interface of assessing cultural knowledge, an essential element of cultural competence, with shared personal practice, a tenet of learning communities. Table 5.1 presents three lanes of information:

- The first column presents a description of assessing cultural knowledge.
- The second column presents a description of shared personal practice.
- The third column represents the interface of the two elements and poses questions designed for culturally proficient learning communities.

You will recall that in Chapter 3, we noted that many educators find shared personal practice frightening. When issues of culture, diversity,

Table 5.1 Assessing Cultural Knowledge Through Shared Personal Practice in Culturally Proficient Learning Communities

Assessing Cultural Knowledge	Shared Personal Practice	Questions to Guide Assessing Cultural Knowledge Through Shared Personal Practice
Extent to which professional learning addresses cultural identity. Professional learning informs learners about their culture, the cultures of others, and the school's culture. Educational gaps are closed through appropriate uses of cultural, linguistic, learning, and communication styles.	Community members give and receive feedback that supports their individual improvement as well as that of the organization.	• How do I conduct individual and group assessments? • In what ways do I develop peer-to-peer support toward specific goals? • In what ways do I/we plan and facilitate intentional professional learning to improve student learning? • In what ways do I continue to learn about my own culture? • In what ways do I/we learn about the cultures of our students? • In what ways do I/we learn about the organizational cultures that exist within the school (e.g., departmental, grade level, staff-faculty)? • In what ways do I/we become aware of how I react to the cultures of the students? • In what ways do I/we learn how the educators and school are viewed from the cultural communities in the school area? • In what ways do I/we learn and use differentiated teaching strategies? • In what ways do I/we learn and use standards-based assessments to improve instruction? • As a learning community, how do we learn about each other and the unique learning needs within our learning community? • As a learning community, in what ways do we share our understanding of our students' various cultures and their learning needs? • In what ways do I clarify my own beliefs about culture and diversity?

and equity are added to school-based discussions, personal insecurities and opportunities for cross-cultural miscommunication are often heightened. It is for these reasons that the intentional addressing of the standards for culturally proficient learning communities serves both the educator community and, as a direct consequence, the students and parents or guardians in our school communities. This approach supports educators directly by addressing the assets and possibilities of the educators and the diverse communities we serve. Educators-helping-educators develop a shared understanding for all staff members' success in meeting the needs of all students becomes the mantra that cascades throughout the schools and district. Sharing personal practice assumes that all teachers can and will learn best strategies in working with all demographic groups. Administrators coach each other to mediate best thinking in creating conditions to support all learners. District office administrators support colleagues to develop their talents and strengths as resources to support changing practice. Sharing our practice means trusting and believing in ourselves, our colleagues, and most of all, our students.

Take a moment and pay particular attention to the guiding questions in the third column of Table 5.1. Which of the questions guide your personal, professional work? Which of the questions guide your school's professional development plan? Which of the questions would, if you chose them to guide your work, represent a growth experience for you? How might you benefit? Which of the questions would guide a growth experience for your school? How might the school benefit? How might students in your school benefit? Use the space below to record your responses to the questions in this section that resonate for you at this time.

_____

_____

_____

_____

_____

Barriers and Breakthroughs: Confronting Inequity Through Collaborative Curiosity

Shared personal practice means learning-community members develop peer-to-peer support toward achieving specific goals and results. Culturally proficient learning community members are willing to examine the influence of the school's organizational structure on the needs of their students. Community members look for ways to set new goals that are in response to and consistent with students', parents', and educators' feedback regarding a policy, program, or procedure. Often, groups get stuck when they first examine data about programs or procedures. Sometimes, members of the group ask questions and make comments that serve as barriers to moving forward. For example, a *barrier question* might feel like an inquisition or an interrogation. Asking *why* and *how* questions may include a judgmental and accusatory voice. Barrier questions usually result in shutting down the conversation and inhibiting positive thinking. *Breakthrough questions,* on the other hand, disturb the environment in ways that invite positive thinking and encourage new ideas. Breakthrough questions have specific characteristics that reduce anxiety and open one's thinking toward possibility. Breakthrough questions (a) are open-ended, with no right or wrong answer; (b) use tentative language, such as "how might you"; (c) use plural language, such as "what are some of the ways"; (d) embed positive intention and possibility, such as "Given your desire for all students to be successful . . ."; and, (e) embed one or more of the Essential Elements of Cultural Proficiency, such as "In what ways might we learn more about our newest students?" Recognizing barrier comments and questions and then posing breakthrough questions is a leadership skill to be developed with the learning community.

Voices From the Field

In Chapter 4, we introduced Maple View as a composite of the many stories we witnessed in our schools across the United States and Canada. Let's join Maple View School District for one of the high school's learning team meetings. Listen for barrier comments and look for opportunities to ask breakthrough questions to move thinking forward in a positive way to better serve students.

Assessing Cultural Knowledge Through Shared Personal Practice

Vignette 1: The Discipline Committee

Pine Hills High School has recently made changes to its discipline policies, particularly the tardy policy. School data indicated high numbers of students late for morning classes. The policy had been to punish students for being late by implementing a "tardy sweep," whereby tardy students were swept up and escorted to the multipurpose room until the first class period was over. Teachers and administrators became concerned about the amount of class time students were missing. Data collected at the end of the semester indicated that the policy was not decreasing tardies. As a matter of fact, the number of tardy students had increased! During semester break, administrators and teacher leaders examined the data and developed a new approach focused on involving teachers, students, and parents. The new tardy policy and procedures assumed students wanted to arrive on time, parents would support the new policy, and teachers would take an active role in contacting parents and students. Administrators developed a system of follow-up where students were part of the overall discipline policy.

Given the new focus on learning communities, the school is having one of the learning communities revisit the changes to see what impact, if any, the new procedures are having on the number of tardy students. To be more inclusive, the new learning community has invited students and parents to participate and share in any new decisions relating to discipline.

Learning Community Leader (LCL):	Well, since we implemented our new tardy policy, the data show tardies have decreased 5%.
Teacher:	That's not much. I'm still missing a lot of kids, especially in first period.
Student 1:	Yeah. I was late the other day and my teacher said she would contact my parents the next day. She did, too. But the teacher didn't want to help me make up any of the material either. I'm hardly ever tardy. I hate to miss my assignments and I hate for my parents to know I was late.
Student 2:	My teachers say they have to teach us "responsibility." What about when the teachers are late? Nothing happens to them. Isn't this a double standard?
Parent:	It's not my child's fault for being late. I have to take part of the responsibility. I have two other children to get to school and we never know when a long train will block our way. We have to cross four train tracks in order to get to school.
LCL:	Ok, now that we have heard from the newest members of our committee . . . .

Breakthrough Questions

The Maple View vignette above is rich with opportunities for deepening the conversation in a manner that represents a culturally proficient learning community. Groups often get stuck in their downward spiral of negative, difficult statements and questions that serve as barriers to moving forward to improve educational practice.

The LCL has the opportunity to ask breakthrough questions to help the group shift to an upward spiral of possibility. What might be some breakthrough questions to address the statements and questions?

The hallmark of breakthrough questions is using language that redirects thinking away from certainty and asking "What's wrong?" to curiosity and asking "What's possible?" The LC members might get stuck trying to solve an all-too-familiar issue about student tardies rather than using this as an opportunity to better serve their students *and* decrease tardies. The following are some examples of breakthrough questions for this community:

LCL: Now that we have heard from the newest members of our committee, what might be some adjustments we could make . . . ?

Given the different perspectives that we've heard today, what might be . . . ?

Hearing these comments from our parents and students, how might we . . . ?

What results or goals might we set for the next round of data collection?

Your turn: What might be additional breakthrough questions for the LCL?

Use Table 5.2 to record your breakthrough questions in response to the vignette characters' statements and questions.

REFLECTIONS

In what ways might being aware of barrier comments assist you as a learning community member? What possibilities do breakthrough questions have for you and your community? How might being more inclusive of parents and students in the learning community impact the conversation? Who are the parents and students invited

Table 5.2   Vignette 1: The Discipline Committee

Barrier Statements and Questions	Breakthrough Questions
What good will it do to talk about student achievement when we know these kids are doing the best they can for who they are?	What might be some things that can support our conversations about how all demographic groups are being served by us?
Student #2: My teachers say they have to teach us "responsibility." What about when the teachers are late? Nothing happens to them. Isn't this a double standard?	Your Breakthrough Question:
Parent: It's not my child's fault for being late. I have to take part of the responsibility. I have two other children to get to school and we never know when a long train will block our way. We have to cross four train tracks in order to get to school.	Your Breakthrough Question:

to the table, and in what ways do they represent the diversity of the educational community?

In what ways has including parents and students in the conversation added shared understanding to the learning community? How might a learning community assess their culture? What might be some implications of bringing diverse voices to a learning community?

Please record your responses in the space below.

_____

_____

_____

_____

Vignette 2: Not the Students We Used to Have

Maple View Middle School implemented a climate study to learn how the educators viewed and experienced the changing population at the school. As the student population had become increasingly diverse, it was apparent that some educators were having a difficult time adjusting to the changes, whereas others were taking the changes in stride. In fact, some of the faculty had truly embraced the changing demographics in ways that insured their success and that of their students.

One of the more poignant responses was received from Mrs. G., a veteran teacher, who penned the following note on her climate study:

> I heard myself saying it one more time as I completed this climate study: "Twenty years ago our student body was so different. The kids' parents attended everything. They sponsored classroom activities and events. The students enjoyed learning. We took students on field trips to universities and out of the country." I let that slip away from me and thought it was gone forever. I decided three years ago that teaching would never be the same. I spent ten years marching down Retirement Lane. How dare students come to high school not knowing how to read and write! How dare we be expected to teach them to do their reading and writing in our content areas! How dare they speak with an accent; worse, how dare they slaughter the English language when they have lived here all their lives!
>
> But let me tell you, I was planning to retire last year and realized by the middle of the year that I could not. It has been a remarkable year; the best I have ever had! I want to thank this petite African American lady who has become the wind beneath my wings. She gave me courage to do what was best for students. She told me that one of the reasons why she is a teacher today is because of a group of us who helped make her who she is today. She said that though she was only 1 of 20 African American students at that time (ten years ago), she knew she would go to the university and become a teacher at this school one day. She never acted as though we were different.
>
> I was convinced that over the past 10 years we, indeed, had a different kind of student. I was convinced students didn't care about learning, so I stopped teaching them and started teaching my subject. I didn't care about them the way I had cared about my students and their parents years ago. I made excuses and "dogged" them in staff lounge conversations. I became a mean, middle-aged lady. I knew I belonged to a special group. We often met and made sure we had nothing positive to say about the students or their parents, and sometimes about ourselves. We felt resentment with no regrets. I heard a recurrent voice in my head that told me, "Just wait for retirement. Then you are free of this mess."

Then, two years ago, several new, young teachers were hired. These new teachers agreed to join a group of about 15 others to attend professional learning for Advancement Via Individualized Development (AVID) and small learning communities (SLCs). One of the new teachers invited me to attend. That has made all the difference! I'm now ready to make my last years as a teacher as excellent as my first years.

My conversation with that new teacher went something like this:

Mrs. G. *(a veteran teacher):*	Why should I attend those workshops? I'm about to retire.
Pulani *(a new teacher):*	Oh, Mrs. G. You'll love it. You used to tell me all the time that you and a group from the school would spend much of the summer learning new things for our classes when I was here as a student. Do you realize you and that group of teachers taught me how to write? You taught me how to gather evidence to support my thinking. You made time so each student belonged to a club where we had debates and showed off our artwork. Would you believe, in my first year in college I had an English professor who asked me who wrote an essay I turned in for an assignment? When I asked, "What do you mean?" She said, "Freshmen students can't write like this. Who wrote your essay"? I was so mad at her. I said, "I came from a school where my teachers taught me these things." I challenged her by saying: "Give me a different assignment. I'll write the essay right here. You'll see." She gave me a different writing assignment. When she read the assignment she admitted it was even better than the first. I took my "A" paper, left her office, ran to the Registrar's Office, dropped her class, and signed up for a sophomore level class and never looked back. It was you, Mrs. G., and Mr. Blake who made us know we could do anything.

When Pulani, the petite African American second year teacher, shared this with me, I was ashamed that I had let my teaching fall to the wayside. My resentment was a reality and I knew now that the reason I enjoyed this past year so much was because of her. I started laughing and told her she reintroduced me to the importance of collegiality and working together, of meeting with teachers from different content areas on a regular basis to discuss our students' needs, that in those meetings with teachers I've known for over 20 years that we have just as much to give as the new teachers, and that both groups put students first again. We imagine incredible things together! I'm surprised that I know every one of my students this year. I talk with each of their parents at least once each quarter.

And a very special thank you to the Climate Study Committee for this opportunity to think back over my decisions and to know why I am staying with what I do well and enjoy—which is teaching!

This note provided hope and encouragement for the Climate Study Committee. One committee member said, "See, 'older' teachers can learn 'new' things about themselves." Members of the committee were truly in the know when they witnessed the closing part of this conversation between the veteran teacher, Mrs. G., and Pulani.

Mrs. G.:   I thank you, Pulani, for inviting me to be on our instructional team, for introducing me to the parent who calls all of our students once a week, even though I call them too, for helping me create fun challenging moments of learning for our students and for ourselves. You introduced me to weekly grade checks and literally took me by the hand when we went to the meeting on that pyramid of interventions and those professional learning sessions. You are a phenomenal young lady. I have so much to say to you and I'll say it in a few words. Thank you for saving me from myself. I love my work. I love my students today just as much as I did when you were my student. I have no intention of retiring soon. These are the best years.

Your Turn: Barrier/Breakthrough Questions

This vignette offers opportunities for deepening the conversation in a manner that represents a culturally proficient learning community. Being mindful of not wanting to get stuck in a downward spiral of negative, difficult statements and questions that serve as barriers to moving forward to improve educational practice, what might be breakthrough questions to address the statements and questions in Table 5.3?

Table 5.3   Vignette 2: Not the Students We Used to Have

Barrier Statements and Questions	Breakthrough Questions
I am sorry, it doesn't matter who is in my classroom, I teach my subject and I teach it well. If it doesn't sink in, it is not my fault!	What might be some ways that you can continue to teach to the standards of your subject area and adapt to the learning styles of your diverse student population?
Mrs. G.: I was convinced that over the past ten years we, indeed, had a different kind of student.	Your Breakthrough Question:
Pulani: It was you, Mrs. G., and Mr. Blake who made us know we could do anything.	Your Breakthrough Question:

What might be additional breakthrough questions for the LCL?

Use Table 5.3 to record your breakthrough questions in response to the vignette characters' statements and questions.

REFLECTION

Pause for a moment and think about the many topics in this vignette—changing demographics, teacher burnout, educational innovations, educator expectations of our students, and sharing personal practice. In what ways do you relate to this vignette? Do you have colleagues who are struggling like Mrs. G., the veteran teacher? What do teachers and other educators new to your school have to say about the climate at your school? In what ways do you assess your cultural knowledge as part of sharing your personal practice? Use the space below to record your responses.

_____

_____

_____

_____

GOING DEEPER: 3 KEYS

What are 3 key learnings from this chapter? What are 3 key quotes or comments from the chapter that resonate with you? What are 3 key questions you now have? Thinking of your role as an educator, how does the information from this chapter cause you to think about your practice? In what ways does this information cause you to think differently about your school or district?

_____

_____

_____

_____

_____

_____

_____

_____

_____

6

Valuing Diversity Is a Reflection of Shared Beliefs, Values, and Vision

The person who is truly effective has the humility and reverence to recognize his own perceptual limitations and to appreciate the rich resources available through interaction with the hearts and minds of other human beings. That person values the differences because those differences add to his knowledge, to his understanding or reality. When we're left to our own experiences, we constantly suffer from a shortage of data.

—Covey (2004), p. 277

Getting Centered

Diversity is prevalent in our society. We cannot *not* have diversity. As you read Stephen Covey's quote, what came to mind? Do all students and adults at your school value diversity? Is diversity viewed as a problem to be solved? Or is diversity viewed as an asset?

Take a moment and listen to yourself at your school when speaking about diversity. Then, take a moment and listen to your colleagues when you hear the variety of voices speaking about diversity. As you reflect on your and their talk, how do you characterize the value for diversity at your school—in grade-level or department meetings, in faculty meetings, during professional development, and in the informal chance encounters that occur as you interact with colleagues? Take a few moments and in the space below, describe how diversity is valued at your school—by you and by your colleagues.

_____

_____

_____

_____

Going Deeper With Cultural Proficiency

This chapter focuses on valuing diversity, an essential element of cultural competence, and its interaction with the tenets of learning communities, including shared beliefs, values, and vision. Table 6.1 presents three lanes of information:

- The first column presents a description of valuing diversity.
- The second column presents a description of beliefs, values, and vision.
- The third column represents the interaction of the two sources of elements and poses questions that lead to culturally proficient learning communities.

When you read the questions in the third column, what thoughts or feelings do you have? In thinking of your role as a professional educator, which of these describe how you approach your work? Which of the questions has caused you to think differently about your work? Do any of the questions appropriately address the culture of your grade level, department, or school? Which ones are they? How could your school use the questions to extend your professional

Table 6.1   Valuing Diversity Through Shared Beliefs, Values, and Vision in Culturally Proficient Learning Communities

Valuing Diversity	*Shared Beliefs, Values, and Vision*	*Questions to Guide Valuing Diversity Through Shared Belief, Values, and Vision*
Extent to which professional learning addresses cultural issues. Professional learning recognizes and meets the needs of multiple cultural, linguistic, learning, and communication styles.	Community members consistently focus on students' learning, which is strengthened by the community's learning.	• In what ways do we acknowledge multiple perspectives? • In what ways do we acknowledge common purpose(s)? • In what ways do we base vision and actions on common assessment results? • In what ways do I demonstrate my value for diversity by aligning what I say with what I do? • In what ways do I/we insure that instructional strategies are differentiated in a manner that values diversity? • In what ways do I/we insure that curricular choices reflect a value for diversity? • In what ways do I/we insure that assessment choices reflect a value for diversity? • In what ways do I insure that my expressions of a value for diversity are consistent even when members of that group are not in the room? • In what ways do I insure that my value for diversity is apparent to our students? • In what ways do I insure that my value for diversity is apparent to our parents/guardians? • In what ways do I/we insure that our learning communities incorporate valuing diversity as a lens for our work?

learning? What might it look like? Please use the space below to record your responses.

_____

_____

_____

_____

Diversity is our society in all of its communities. One of our colleagues noted recently that if your school has more than one student, you have diversity. Our school communities are comprised of men and women, boys and girls, people of different faiths, people with different abilities, and people of different sexual orientations. Our school communities are made up of people from diverse racial, ethnic, national, and language-dominant groups.

Similarly, our schools are a mix of organizational cultures. One of the organizational challenges in newly developing learning communities is how to meld the cultures of grade level and departmental units with shared beliefs, values, and vision for the school in a way that promotes unity and individuality. When successful, we have a both-and, not an either-or, world. It is a rare elementary school administrator who fails to recognize that second grade team meetings feel differently than do fourth grade team meetings. At the secondary level, an administrator notices the science department meeting tone is often different from the social sciences subject area meetings. The same secondary administrator notices the interdisciplinary, cross-grade-level team meeting tone is very different when parents, students, and other community members are present.

The fact that these four school groups do things differently is a manifestation of their organizational cultures. There is no right or wrong way; they are just different from one another.

Differences can often be viewed as the root of problems. Too often, the terms *different* or *diversity* are code words for people of color. Diversity training, or equity work, usually incorporates learning about issues of gender, race, ethnicity, language, faith, ableness, and sexual orientation. To that we say a resounding Yes! However, that is not enough. When the door to diversity is opened, we are compelled as educators to be receptive to the wider meanings of culture in order that we may focus on the issues that are most pressing at our schools. Being open to these wider meanings for culture will, in fact, be moments for disturbing the system that has been unaware of or unwilling to address inequities or lack of access within the school or district.

Valuing diversity is seemingly inherent for some of our colleagues and is evident in their personal and professional relationships, their approach to instruction and curriculum, and in how they speak about their students. However, for others of us, valuing diversity is an intentional act in which choice, too often made under the duress of poorly conceived professional development, guides us in learning about cultures different from ours; in learning differentiated approaches to curriculum, instruction, and assessment; and in recognizing that we have a moral responsibility to teach the students who come into our schools each and every day. So what is our obligation to initiate and support deep, sincere, adult learning and commitment that honors curiosity and disturbances?

One way to fulfill this obligation is by engaging in professional learning that values diversity through articulated beliefs and a vision that recognizes and meets the needs of multiple cultural, linguistic, learning, and communication styles. These beliefs, values, and visions embrace the students, their parents or guardians, the community served by the school, and the educators and staff that comprise the school as partners in the educational enterprise. Schools that value diversity as a core component of their articulated beliefs, values, and vision

- acknowledge multiple perspectives,
- acknowledge common purpose(s), and
- base vision and actions on common assessment results.

Voices From the Field

Let us return to Maple View and listen in on their conversations as a way to extend our understanding of valuing diversity and shared beliefs, values, and vision. Community members consistently focus on students' learning, which is strengthened by the community's learning.

Vignette 3: Problem-Based Learning (PBL)

Maple View's vision statement includes these words: "We envision our students as lifelong learners, well prepared for the workplace or college." To operationalize this vision, a new focus for Sam Brewer, as Maple View's new superintendent, is to bring greater relevancy to the curriculum. He and curriculum leaders from each school established a long-range goal to build a library of integrated, problem-based learning lessons that teachers will use in alignment with the current elementary pacing guides. To begin, a small team will work with a consultant over the course of the year. In the following year, the district plans to expand the number of lessons and have all teachers begin using lessons from the new online library. Some teachers are ready to move forward quickly, while others want nothing to do with adding this to their full plates. How might being inclusive from the beginning impact their success later in the process? Here's a recent conversation among the external "problem-based strategies" educational consultant, an MVSD professional development specialist, and an MVSD teacher.

Consultant:	Knowing your goal is for all teachers to ultimately integrate these lessons into their curriculum, what are some things you are worried about?
Teacher A:	Everyone is exhausted and reluctant to start something new. Actually, I'm not sure there is much more we can do!
Professional Development Specialist:	Yeah, I get discouraged myself. I'm not sure where to start.
Consultant:	What might be some ways you can focus on your goal of being more inclusive of others from the very beginning of our work?
Teacher B:	Well, we can share the lessons at the grade-level team meetings.
Teacher A:	That's true. We have our learning-teams meeting every week to look at our common assessment data. We also examine our curriculum, look at where our students are not doing well, and identify strategies that work with struggling students.
Consultant:	Since some teachers will be implementing these lessons and others won't, even though they are covering the same standards, how might this change the conversation of the learning teams?
Teacher A:	Well, we could look at our students' data to see if the PBL lessons are having an impact on our students' success.

Professional Development Specialist:	We could even think about how we might get input from teachers who aren't writing the lessons as to how they might contribute their expertise or insights as we develop the lesson.
Teacher B:	Yeah, that way they'll have a better understanding of the lessons for when they implement them next year, especially if they've contributed in some way.
Consultant:	So seeking input from other perspectives and being inclusive might smooth the road for when this goes full scale throughout the district.

Breakthrough Questions

This vignette, similar to those in the previous chapter, has many opportunities for deepening the conversation in a manner that represents a culturally proficient learning community. Being mindful of not wanting to get stuck in a downward spiral of negative, difficult statements and questions that serve as barriers to moving forward to improve educational practice, what might be breakthrough questions to address the statements and questions in Table 6.2?

Table 6.2　Vignette 3: Problem-Based Learning

Barrier Statements and Questions	*Breakthrough Questions*
How can we focus on problem-based learning when we know some of these kids, and we know who they are, can't even read at grade level?	*How might we use the data we have about student reading levels to inform the development of problem-based learning activities?*
Teacher: *Everyone is exhausted and reluctant to start something new. Actually, I'm not sure there is much more we can do!*	*Your Breakthrough Question:*
Specialist: *Yeah, I get discouraged, too. I'm not sure where to start?*	*Your Breakthrough Question:*

REFLECTION

What might be some outcomes as a result of the team providing opportunities for others to contribute their knowledge and expertise to the process of developing the PBL lessons? Who might be some other stakeholders the learning team might want to engage in this process? What are some guidelines you might use to identify who needs to be at the table? What other contexts might you consider for being more inclusive in decision making? Please use the space below to record your responses.

_____

_____

_____

_____

Vignette 4: Personal Identities

Maple View High School was in the midst of developing learning teams. One of the emerging issues was faculty awareness about student issues that had not been prevalent even just a few years ago. One team member spoke up at the beginning of a recent learning team meeting, "How can we be expected to teach the kids who don't even speak English or even know how to read?" Another teacher commented in response, "You're right, of course; but we are expected to be 'politically correct' these days about how we talk about these kids." These comments led to silence by some team members and equally negative comments by other team members.

As the learning team continued to meet, one member asked the group, "What is the purpose of this learning team anyway? What are we hoping to learn that will make us better teachers?" The team members were struggling with issues of diversity in their school and their common mission for improved student achievement. The mathematics teacher, Mrs. Milanovich, was not prepared for the unexpected dynamics that surrounded the planned 30-minute conversation. When the administrator, Ms. Lopez, entered the room, Mrs. Milanovich said her learning team was dealing with some real challenges. Ms. Lopez acknowledged her concerns and agreed to address the team's concerns at a later time. She reminded the team that the student performances were about to begin. Mrs. Milanovich walked with Ms. Lopez over to the multipurpose room for the student presentations.

As the room began to fill with students, educators, and parents gathering to hear the students' presentations, Zenovah, one of the 10th-grade students, entered with her iPod plugs in her ears. Nodding her head to a beat that only she could enjoy, she waved to different folks about the room as she sat at the table in front with an empty chair on either side of her.

The faculty learning-team members were excited about the students' work and the opportunity to show parents and community members how well the students were doing. Zenovah, one of their top students, was presenting a simulation of her group's project to the team, members of the city's fire department and waste disposal company, her parents, the university environmental scientist with his graduate student, and a few of her buddies. The local newspaper was scheduled to interview Zenovah's project team next week. Everybody on the team wanted to be sure they were all on the same page when the cameras rolled on Wednesday, so the afternoon simulation was important. Zenovah seemed to be the only one who was relaxed and confident.

Two women entered the room three or four minutes before the presentation began and waved to Zenovah. Zenovah jumped up from her table and ran over, hugging both. As she returned to her chair, she pulled out the chairs on either side of her and said, "Mom, sit here."

Mrs. Milanovich, sitting two chairs from Zenovah, leaned over and said, "I think I met the lady coming to this chair a few weeks ago. I thought she was your mother." Zenovah said, "They both are my mothers. They just got married last month. Now I have two mothers."

Mrs. Milanovich turned her head, took a deep breath, and held it as she heard Zenovah begin the simulation. The issues Mrs. Milanovich had begun to share with the administrator just a few moments earlier faded into the background. She was trying to understand her reaction to Zenovah's parents.

Breakthrough Questions

Consider that you are a member of this learning team and that the members of the fire department, waste disposal company, the university scientists, and Zenovah and her parents have left. Mrs. Milanovich and your other colleagues have remained to discuss future plans. Being mindful of not wanting to get stuck in a downward spiral of negative, difficult statements and questions that serve as barriers to moving forward to improve educational practice, what might be breakthrough questions to address the statements and questions in Table 6.3?

Table 6.3   Vignette 4: Personal Identities

Barrier Statements and Questions	Breakthrough Questions
I can't believe that those two women would be so brazen as to come to this important meeting and flaunt their chosen lifestyle!	How do you describe Zenovah's demeanor when her two mothers entered the classroom?
Team Member A: I found it interesting that Zenovah seemed to be proud of having her parents with her to witness her presentation. My being bothered was that I didn't know how to act in their presence given their openness and directness.	Your Breakthrough Question:
Team Member B: We are expected to be "politically correct" these days about how we talk about these kids.	Your Breakthrough Question:

REFLECTION

In what ways is the sexual orientation of Zenovah's parents an issue for a learning community? How might information about parental sexual orientation inform a learning community? What was getting in the way of the mission and goals of the learning team in this vignette? As you think about your school community, in what ways would information about various definitions of family benefit you and your colleagues and, in turn, your students? How might all students benefit from this information? In what ways is valuing diversity reflected in your district's vision statement, shared beliefs, and values?

_____

_____

_____

_____

_____

_____

GOING DEEPER: 3 KEYS

What are 3 key learnings from this chapter? What are 3 key quotes or comments from the chapter that resonate with you? What are 3 key questions you now have? Thinking of your role as an educator, how does the information from this chapter cause you to think about your practice? In what ways does this information cause you to think differently about your school or district?

_____

_____

_____

_____

_____

_____

7

Managing the Dynamics of Difference Through Collaboration

The mix of values in a society provides multiple vantage points from which to view reality. Conflict and heterogeneity are resources for social learning. Although people may not share one another's values, they may learn vital information that would ordinarily be lost to view without engaging the perspectives of those who challenge them.

—Heifetz, 1994, p. 35

Getting Centered

Managing the dynamics of difference is a way to describe handling conflict that carries at least one important caveat. Conflict that arises from cross-cultural issues often increases the perceived risks and causes people who behave somewhat rationally in nonculturally-based instances of conflict to lose self-confidence, a sense of control, or the ability to be impartial. In contrast, when a value for diversity exists at the personal and school levels, managing conflict is viewed and experienced as a natural part of communication and problem solving.

As you read Heifetz's (1994) quote, what comes to mind for you? Take a few moments and think about how you respond to issues that arise from cultural differences. How do you think you respond? How would you like to respond? As you think about issues that surface within your school, how does your school community respond to issues that are based in cultural differences? How does your school respond to culturally-based issues that arise from the neighborhoods that your school serves?

Please use the space below to record your responses.

_____

_____

_____

_____

What Difference Does Difference Make?

In our everyday lives, we can be animated when disagreeing about seemingly trivial things, such as who is better, the Mets versus the Yankees, or Jay versus Dave, or who is the best rock singer. Even with fervent feelings about our choices, we can consider others' perspectives. When we enter the professional arena, we often strenuously disagree over curricular choices, instructional approaches, the value of professional development, or union leadership. Yet even within emotionally charged professional discussions, we can maintain a sense of personal efficacy and professional decorum. We often resolve the professional conflicts by agreeing that we disagree and then walk away with smiles.

In contrast to nonculturally-based conflict, conflict based in cultural differences often creates negative reactions. When our students divide along cultural lines, we take note and become concerned. When our faculty and staff are polarized along cultural lines, we feel the stress. When the community that our school serves is culturally different from the culture of the educators, miscommunication may ensue and create strained relationships.

In our schools today, cultural divides may be about issues with expressed or underlying racial, ethnic, language, gender, social class, faith, ableness, or sexual orientation themes. When conflict is present, it may be hidden due to the avoidance mechanisms employed in the school. Most people can feel the tension that arises from avoidance, and in situations such as those described in the previous paragraph, feelings of discomfort are manifest throughout the school. The opposite is also true. When a value for diversity exists, managing issues that arise from cultural differences are surfaced, explored, and resolved as part of ongoing communication, problem-solving processes, and collaboration.

Going Deeper With Cultural Proficiency

This chapter continues the focus on the Essential Elements of Cultural Proficiency by highlighting the management of the dynamics of difference and its relationships with the attribute of learning communities' shared and supportive leadership, which is most often characterized as collaboration. Table 7.1 presents three lanes of information:

Table 7.1   Managing the Dynamics of Difference and Shared and Supportive Leadership in Culturally Proficient Learning Communities

Managing the Dynamics of Difference	*Shared and Supportive Leadership/Collaboration*	*Questions to Guide Managing the Dynamics of Difference Through Collaboration*
Extent to which professional learning promotes and models the use of inquiry and dialogue related to multiple perspectives. Professional learning opportunities incorporate multiple perspectives on relevant topics and build capacity for dialogue about conflict related to difference and diversity.	Administrators and community members hold shared power and authority for making decisions.	• In what ways do we foster discussions about race, gender, sexual orientation, socioeconomics, and faith as related to the needs of our community? • In what ways are our decision-making processes transparent and subject to change based on community needs? • In what ways do we foster alternative narratives in the classroom and in the formal curriculum? • In what ways do we foster alternative narratives and views in school meetings? • In what ways do we foster alternative narratives in parent and community meetings? • In what ways do we use assessment data to inform successful and unsuccessful practices?

- The first column presents a description of managing the dynamics of difference.
- The second column presents a description of shared and supportive leadership or collaboration.
- The third column represents the interaction of the two sources of elements and poses questions to guide culturally proficient learning communities.

Please take a few moments and read again the questions in the third column of Table 7.1. What thoughts or feelings occur to you? Which of the questions guide how you approach your work at the school? Which questions are present in the ongoing discussions among faculty and staff at your school? Which questions pose the opportunity for further learning for you and for your school? The space below is for you to record your comments, thoughts, questions, and feelings.

_____

_____

_____

_____

Collaborative Leadership

As presented in Table 7.1, managing the dynamics of difference in a collaborative community can be assessed by the extent to which professional learning promotes and models the use of inquiry and dialogue related to multiple perspectives. Professional learning opportunities incorporate multiple perspectives on relevant topics and build capacity for dialogue about conflict related to difference and diversity. Collaboratively managing the dynamics of difference means

- openly fostering discussions about race, gender, sexual orientation, socioeconomics, and faith as related to the needs of the community; and
- ensuring that decision-making processes are transparent and subject to change based on community needs.

Leading and facilitating collaborative learning are learned leadership skills. Hargraves (in Hord and Sommers, 2008) emphasized that leaders, both formal and informal, of professional learning communities are initiators not merely reactors and managers. He also said that "all leadership involves opposition and the necessity of dealing with it" (p. xi). The dynamics of acknowledging conflict as a natural part of organizational life presents leaders with opportunities to expect diversity of opinions, experiences, and perspectives. Complexity theory identified diversity as necessary for organizational growth and development and connected personal learning that occurs in professional communities to how an individual's personal learning affects the larger community. Zellermayer and Margolin (2005), through their study of critical events, identified factors that sustain evolving communities:

- Colleagues who enable and coordinate group learning lead the change process.
- Participants are provided time and a place to talk about their work.
- Participants are provided a platform to make public presentations about their interpretations of the change process.
- Learning takes place among diverse points of view that rarely reach consensus.
- There is recognition of multiple possibilities for communal learning.
- In time, participants learn of the need to collaborate with others.
- Participants, in time, engage in reflection that includes recognition of how their value systems are challenged.
- Participants are not able to change others, but as they change, the community as a whole changes.
- A climate of risk taking is fostered that includes encouraging differences of opinion.
- A climate of safety is fostered for those threatened by the change process.
- Participants are provided the opportunity to focus in on their emotions and, simultaneously, view their learning in a larger theoretical context.

The change process benefits from having a facilitator who can identify sources of resistance and collaboration and uses the resulting dissonance to spark learning and group development (pp. 32–33).

As we reflect on these factors that sustain evolving communities, we next listen in on learning community conversations at Maple View.

Voices From the Field

Returning to Maple View, we find two vignettes that illustrate the dynamics of managing differences and collaboration.

Vignette 5: Equity of Access

The Maple View School District continues to work toward providing equitable and greater access to rigorous curriculum for all high school students. The superintendent has invited his colleagues from the local university to join the learning team and contribute information relating to the university's new Social Justice program, which aligns well with the district's Cultural Proficiency initiatives. The superintendent's intent is to bring greater awareness of the contextual issues of equity of access. He wants Maple View educators to examine their own viewpoints and biases, particularly when developing criteria for admission to rigorous curriculum.

We enter the vignette about 30 minutes into the session, and we witness some of the district learning team members highly engaged and passionate while others are disengaged and showing dissatisfaction with the way the conversation is going. The professors had been following the Cultural Proficiency work being undertaken in Maple View and decided that the learning community would benefit from information on issues of racism with a particular focus on how people benefit from systemic racism.

LC Member 1: Let me see if I understand what you are saying, Dr. Jenkins. It is your viewpoint and study that we too often focus on how people are negatively impacted by issues of racism and that we turn a blind eye to how people benefit from the very practices that penalize or demonize others?

Dr. Jenkins: Precisely! And it is important to point out that we are not talking about intentional bigotry or racism.

LC Member 1: Please stay with me for a moment while I see if I get what you are saying. Would this be a good example? Say a person couldn't vote due to their race or ethnicity. Does that act of racism increase the value of my vote?

Dr. Jenkins: Yes, that is an appropriate example. An educational example would be that a curriculum that fails to include the authentic contributions of people of color to our history, literature, and sciences is a curriculum that communicates that white people are highly valued and important while the omission of people of color tells all students that people of color had little or no part in making our society as it is today.

LC Member 2:   Wait! Wait! I have to comment on this political correctness parade that is making its way through this room! Are you trying to tell me that just because I don't know about "multicultural interpretations" of curriculum that I am somehow deficient or even racist? I have worked hard for everything I have learned and earned to be an educator in this school for all of our students. I really don't like the insinuation that there is something wrong with me!

Breakthrough Questions

This vignette presents a familiar conundrum for those presenting material that challenges prevalent beliefs, yet it has many opportunities for deepening the conversation in a manner that is indicative of culturally proficient learning communities. Not wanting to get stuck in a downward spiral of negative, difficult statements and questions that serve as barriers to moving forward to improve educational practice, what might be breakthrough questions to address the statements and questions in Table 7.2?

Table 7.2   Vignette 5: Equity of Access

Barrier Statements and Questions	Breakthrough Questions
I have worked hard for everything I have learned and earned to be an educator in this school for all of our students. I really don't like the insinuation that there is something wrong with me!	In what ways do you see that Dr. Jenkins or any of the rest of us have blamed you or insinuated there is something wrong with you as a person or as an educator?
LC Member 1: Hey, lighten up and stow the defensiveness!	Your Breakthrough Question:
LC Member 2: I am so tired of coming to these sessions to be blamed for things that happened years ago!	Your Breakthrough Question:

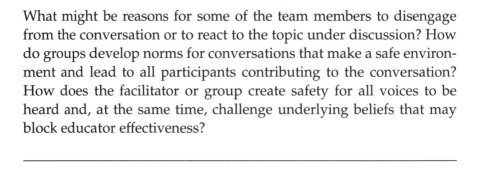

REFLECTION

What might be reasons for some of the team members to disengage from the conversation or to react to the topic under discussion? How do groups develop norms for conversations that make a safe environment and lead to all participants contributing to the conversation? How does the facilitator or group create safety for all voices to be heard and, at the same time, challenge underlying beliefs that may block educator effectiveness?

_____

_____

_____

_____

Vignette 6: Rigor and Relevancy?

MVSD office administrators are aware that the state now requires all students to take at least one career technical education (CTE) class during their high school experience and all schools to provide on graduation diplomas recognition for students completing a 3-year sequence of CTE courses. The superintendent wants to ensure mutual commitment from the staff and community on this top-down mandate and approaches it as an opportunity for increased collaboration among the high school leadership team, with particular emphasis on bringing together the career technical and the core subject high school faculty. He sees that by focusing on relevance, real-world connections, and twenty-first century learning that the students in the school could benefit from this otherwise mandated curricular change. He wants to build on the current strengths of the school, address local economic needs, and align with current certificate programs offered at the local colleges.

Superintendent Brewer convenes a meeting to examine the possibilities. He invites the Pine Hills High School leadership team, including representatives from career technical and core academic high school teachers. He also invites representatives from five local businesses, two members of the local workforce development agency, a nearby community college instructor, and a state university professor. The superintendent and members of the leadership team recognize that with such a diverse group, differences in belief systems and dialogue style could emerge.

Superintendent: Thank you all for being here today. I believe we all want the same outcome—high achieving

	graduates who are well prepared for post-secondary education and the workforce. Our purpose as a learning community is to see how we can improve our students' readiness for life after high school by collaborating and learning from and with one another.
Teacher:	We've already met as a staff and decided how we want to respond to this mandate. Things are working well for us now, just as they always have. Of course, we want to keep our favorite courses, who wouldn't?
Counselor:	My daughter will be a student here in two years and the existing programs are not ready for her. I appreciate that we are all here today. I feel that we have the option to move from our current reality to something different . . . from what we already have that works for only 12% of our kids. I want to continue doing what I've always done, but that will not be enough for her to be ready for postsecondary challenges. The rest of my guidance department team would rather that we say one thing, close our doors, turn on our computers, wait until year's end, schedule our kids as always, and keep things the way they always have been—programs for a few, but certainly not for all.
Community College Representative:	Well, we already have in place our certificate programs. It's a huge process to change these and to get them approved by all the necessary committees and professional boards.
Local Business Representative:	I need graduates as employees who have strong "soft skills," who can interact effectively in a team, and who are self-directed. I don't want to have to always be telling them what to do and how to do it. I am here to find out if these soft skills for basic, workplace communication skills are being taught schoolwide.

Breakthrough Questions

This vignette presents an interesting mix of different perspectives on how the issue at hand, that of a mandated course intended to improve students' preparedness for the world of work and school accountability, might be addressed collaboratively. As with previous vignettes, if you don't want to get stuck in a downward spiral of negative, difficult statements and questions that serve as barriers to moving forward to improving educational practice, what might be some breakthrough questions to address the statements and questions in Table 7.3?

Table 7.3   Vignette 6: Breakthrough Questions for Managing Dynamics of Difference and Collaboration

Barrier Statements and Questions	Breakthrough Questions
Teacher: *We've already met as a staff and decided how we want to respond to this mandate. Of course, we want to keep our favorite courses, who wouldn't?*	*In what ways do you see that discussion today with our colleagues from the community college and local businesses inform your curriculum and your favorite courses?*
Community College Rep: *Well, we already have in place our certificate programs. It's a huge process to change these and to get them approved by all the necessary committees and professional boards.*	*Your Breakthrough Question:*
Local Business Rep: *I need employees who have strong soft skills, who can interact effectively in a team, and who are self-directed. I don't want to have to always be telling them what to do and how to do it. I am here to find out why these human communication skills are not being taught.*	*Your Breakthrough Question:*

REFLECTION

How do you react to the rapid-fire and different responses from the three speakers? Does this type of response occur in your school meetings? How do you react at the time? What are your feelings—do you withdraw from the conversation, or do you help facilitate the conversation? What would you like to do in situations such as this? What is the role of collaborative leadership in this situation? Please use the space below to record your feelings and thoughts.

_____

_____

_____

_____

GOING DEEPER: 3 KEYS

What are 3 key learnings from this chapter? What are 3 key quotes or comments from the chapter that resonate with you? What are 3 key questions you now have? Thinking of your role as an educator, how does the information from this chapter cause you to think about your practice? In what ways does this information cause you to think differently about your school or district?

_____

_____

_____

_____

_____

_____

_____

_____

_____

8

Adapting to Diversity Through Supportive and Shared Conditions

The courses, the texts, and the experiences all are aimed at addressing some alleged pathology on the part of the students, their families, their communities, and/or their cultures. The school quickly imperializes the space of normalcy, and any students who do not conform to that space are thought to have abnormalities that emanate from outside of the school in the "dangerous, chaotic worlds" of their families and communities.

—Ladson-Billings, 2005, p. 19

Getting Centered

Adapting to diversity involves recognizing that our school communities are composed of many cultural groups. In Chapter 6, we noted that we cannot *not* have diversity. When educators and their schools successfully adapt to diversity, a commitment is made to educate the students who are in the school, not the students who used to be there or who we might wish were there. As you read Gloria Ladson-Billings' (2005) quote, what thoughts, feelings, or questions arise for you? Must students adapt to the way schools are designed and structured? What must schools do to adapt to the needs of students and their families? What are the traditional conditions in place at your school that might exclude some students from access or engagement? What might be some conditions or structures in place to support you and your colleagues adapting to the changing community? Please use the space below for your responses and comments.

_____

_____

_____

_____

We, the authors, have had the repeated experience of being with educators at all levels—elementary school, middle/junior high school, high school, and college/university—who have remarked that the school just isn't the same as it used to be. In due time, voices emerge that repeat the refrains listed above—these kids aren't like the ones who used to be here or I wish we had different students. As stark as these comments may be, when educators who make such comments are pressed, they find that the good old days are not nearly as rosy as remembered. More important, such comments often draw light to the instructors who are resisting their own learning and how they must change themselves in order to be effective with the new demographic groups of students. This also tells us that, as a profession, we have yet to acknowledge that not all demographic groups of students are new. Many students have been in our system for decades; however, it is as if we have recently acknowledged their presence, their needs, or the contributions they have made to our new learnings and understandings.

Learning about new cultural groups of students should be the core of what we do as educators. Learning about our students must be on par with learning effective ways to teach, or learning new content, or acquiring new technology skills.

Oftentimes, the perceived "new demographic groups" of students that have emerged because of accountability processes are not so new after all. In fact, many of these new or emerging demographic groups of students have been with us all along, and the recent push for greater accountability has made these groups visible for the first time. Current emphases on socioeconomic status, English language learners, and cognitive and physical abilities have now brought these groups on par with race, gender, and student groups who have been historically well served in our schools.

Our heightened emphasis today is on teaching groups of students who had been rendered somewhat invisible by past assessment and accountability practices. Until very recently, prevalent practices focused narrowly on schoolwide test scores. Now we have the opportunity to couple inclusive demographic group assessments with the changing demographics of neighborhoods in many of our communities in Canada and the United States. Today, multiple assessments, culturally relevant instructional practices, and standards-based curriculum provide great opportunities to learn knowledge and develop skills that will prepare us to be more effective at educating all learners.

Going Deeper With Cultural Proficiency

Culturally proficient learning communities use data to inform the assessment of current policies and practices, to discover what is not effective, and to replace what is not effective with policies and practices intended to be more appropriate to the new communities. This learn-unlearn-relearn process brings with it the opportunity to hear multiple voices and experiences of colleagues when we discuss and discover how to better serve our students. Professional learning community members provide high quality learning experiences for all teachers and community members.

Undoubtedly, you and your school have experienced some of the dynamics described above. Either your school's focus on heightened accountability, or your school's changing student demographics, or both has caused you to look outside yourself for support and assistance in being even more effective than you have been in the past.

This chapter continues the focus on the Essential Elements of Cultural Proficiency by emphasizing adapting to diversity and its relationships with the attribute of learning communities' supportive and shared conditions. Table 8.1 presents three lanes of information:

- The first column presents a description of adapting to diversity.

- The second column presents a description of supportive and shared conditions.

- The third column presents the interaction of the two sources of elements and poses questions to guide culturally proficient learning communities.

Table 8.1 Adapting to Diversity Through Supportive and Shared
Conditions in Culturally Proficient Learning Communities

Adapting to Diversity	Supportive and Shared Conditions	Questions to Guide Adapting to Diversity Through Supportive and Shared Leadership
Extent to which professional learning facilitates change to meet the needs of the community. Professional learning opportunities use data to drive change to better meet the needs of a diverse community.	*Structural factors* provide time, facility, resources, and policies to support collaboration. *Relational factors* support the community's human and interpersonal development, openness, truth telling, and attitudes of respect and care among the members.	• In what ways do I teach appropriate communication skills to allow for multiple voices and experiences? • In what ways do I develop adaptive practices to support newcomers as well as veteran community members? • In what ways do I keep apprised of the changing demographics of our school, community, region, state, and country? • In what ways do I incorporate cultural knowledge into the classroom, irrespective of the demographic composition of the classroom, school, or district? • How do I/we learn about the cultures and histories of new demographic groups of students who enroll in the school? • In what ways does our learning community advocate for equity when resources are limited?

Please review the guiding questions in the third column of Table 8.1. What thoughts or feelings occur to you? Which of the questions guides your work at the school? Which questions are present in the ongoing discussions among faculty and staff at your school? Which questions pose the opportunity for further learning for you and for your school? The space below is for you to record your comments, thoughts, questions, and feelings.

_____

_____

_____

_____

Adapting to Diversity Through Supportive and Shared Conditions

Supportive and shared conditions are exemplified by

- structural factors that provide time, facility, resources, and policies to support collaboration;
- relational factors that support the community's human and interpersonal development, openness, truth telling, and attitudes of respect, care, and a sense of shared responsibility among the members; and
- time, trust, tasks, targets, and talk, which are all hallmarks of learning communities. Teams of educators, parents, and members of the external school community come together to create conditions for focusing on improved student performance. Members of the learning community need time to work together to identify goals and targets for teachers and students.

The productivity of these teams is dependent on relational trust and respect for all members of the community. Team leaders take responsibility to identify and include new members to the school community and provide support structures to enhance conversations focused on adapting to the changing needs of the community.

By now, you are familiar with the vignettes and opportunities to identify barrier comments and questions and create breakthrough questions. As you read the vignettes that follow and create your breakthrough questions, pay particular attention to the structural and relational factors that support the learning community's adapting to diversity.

Voices From the Field

Vignette 7: Integrating AP/Honors and Career Technical Classes

The state passed a law requiring all students to take at least one career technical education (CTE) class during their high school experience. Since West Side High School is moving structurally into small learning environments, the principal sees an opportunity for the new learning teams to bring greater collaboration, relevance, real-world connections, and twenty-first century learning to the students' high school experience. In the following dialogue, core academic and career technical education teachers examine this new information. Differences in belief systems emerge immediately. The teachers represent Advanced Placement (AP) classes, Core Academic Programs (CAP), and Career Technical Education (CTE).

AP Teacher: We already have an impacted curriculum in our honors and AP classes. I don't see how we could ever bring in more requirements on top of what we're already doing. Kids need every minute in order to score well on the AP tests. Besides, our kids don't need to take CTE classes anyways. They're going off to college when they graduate.

CAP Teacher: I agree. I don't see any need to connect our classes to CTE classes. Those are totally different kids who take CTE classes. Our core classes are what the students need for graduation credits. Of course, some kids just can't make it in core classes. What should we do with them?

CTE Teacher: Hey, wait a minute. I thought the purpose of our meeting was to see how we could collaborate and integrate our curricula, not whether or not we have an option in doing this. We're all going to need to change what we're doing. I need to bring more rigor into my curriculum, you need to bring more relevance into yours. I think we can take the best of both and really help our kids.

Principal: Ok, ok, enough said. How are we going to move beyond our own special interests to better serve all students?

Breakthrough Questions

This vignette presents an often familiar clash of interests. At the same time, the vignette has opportunities for deepening the conversation in a manner that is indicative of culturally proficient learning communities. Not wanting to get stuck in a downward spiral of negative, difficult statements and questions that serve as barriers to moving forward to improve educational practice, what might be breakthrough questions to address the statements and questions in Table 8.2?

Table 8.2 Vignette 7: Integrating AP/Honors and Career Technical Classes

Barrier Statements and Questions	Breakthrough Questions
AP Teacher: *We already have an impacted curriculum in our honors and AP classes. I don't see how we could ever bring in more requirements on top of what we're already doing. Kids need every minute in order to score well on the AP tests. Besides, our kids don't need to take CTE classes anyways. They're going off to college when they graduate.*	*In what ways might our current curriculum and courses already address the CTE requirement?*
CTE Teacher: *Hey, wait a minute. I thought the purpose of our meeting was to see how we can collaborate and integrate our curricula, not whether or not we have an option in doing this. We're all going to need to change what we're doing. I need to bring more rigor into my curriculum, you need to bring more relevancy into yours. I think we can take the best of both and really help our kids.*	*Your Breakthrough Question:*

REFLECTION

What might be some beliefs that underlie the thinking of each of the learning team members? When you hear yourself or colleagues speak disapprovingly about our kids, how do you respond? How would you like to respond? Please use the space below to record your feelings, thoughts, and comments.

_____

_____

_____

_____

Vignette 8: Common Planning Time

Maple View School District has provided resources to support common planning time at all schools. Several teachers at the middle schools have decided to make the best use of the time by personalizing ways to enhance learning experiences and expand how they work collaboratively across disciplines to better meet the needs of their students. Several teachers are experts in providing feedback and receiving feedback about their students' work. However, some teachers do not see the benefit of structuring common planning or team time. A science teacher and a social studies teacher engage in a conversation about the work in their small learning community:

Tocraski: Hey, Owolbe, there's a problem-based-learning (PBL) staff training for us in three weeks. Two of us from our small learning community (SLC) team are thinking about going to the training. Did you respond to the e-mail? Are you planning to go? We could sure use your help in getting our five-week lesson going.

Owolbe: You know, those kinds of sessions always leave me cold. I'm not a "touchy-feely" kind of person and they always try to get folks to collaborate with each other. What's up with that?

Tocraski: Well, you know the counselor over at the high school has found three businesses in the area that are interested in a PBL. She is the school's Career Technology Counselor. Our university partner will be there, too—you know, Dr. Kanter. The project is issues-based. You know how our students love debates. The team could use your help. This will be our third issues-based project this year without you. The team asked me to invite you again.

Owolbe: You know, I would like to, but I have another engagement. I can't make it. When you get back, tell me about it. Anyway, I hate to miss my classes.

Tocraski made a mental note of how energized he was when he met with the high school counselor, local business representatives, the university professor from the social sciences department, and his SLC teacher colleagues. He wondered why Owolbe never attended the sessions. This was the first year for school members to have common planning time. He appreciated that they were able to talk with one another about students they had in class and compare notes on challenges, successful strategies, and experiences in working with the students' parents. He saw Owolbe in the faculty lounge and went to him and began describing the success of the first PBL meeting.

Owolbe: *(interrupting)* Yeah, yeah, I know. But my students need me. They would create havoc for any substitute. I really don't trust the students or the substitute. I'll prepare my lectures for my classes and get ahead while you're away. I've had nothing but trouble all year long. You know, these kids don't get it. I give them the best lectures in school. They get a variety of worksheets to complete. I work hard on those handouts every night, nearly three hours every night. They don't appreciate much of anything else. As a matter of fact, they are doing the best they can, I guess. You know how hard school is for those kids from downtown. So you see, I can't go to that inservice. I can't miss my classes. My kids need me.

Breakthrough Questions

Do the issues in this vignette sound familiar to you? This vignette has opportunities for deepening the conversation in a manner that is indicative of culturally proficient learning communities. To avoid getting stuck in a downward spiral of negative, difficult statements and questions that serve as barriers to moving forward to improve educational practice, what might be breakthrough questions to address the statements and questions in Table 8.3?

Table 8.3 Vignette 8: Common Planning Time

Barrier Statements and Questions	Breakthrough Questions
Owolbe (social studies teacher): *You know, those kinds of sessions always leave me cold. I'm not a "touchy-feely" kind of person and they always try to get folks to collaborate with each other. What's up with that?*	*How might others benefit from your experiences as a teacher?*
Owolbe: *You know, I would like to, but I have another engagement. I can't make it. When you get back, tell me about it. Anyway, I hate to miss my classes.*	*Your Breakthrough Question:*

REFLECTION

How do you describe the underlying issues in this vignette? What do you see as the adapting to diversity issues? Given that common planning time and professional development resources have been allocated, what do you see as next steps? When you hear yourself or colleagues make comments like those of Owolbe, how do you respond? How would you like to respond? Please use the space below to record your feelings, thoughts, and comments.

_____

_____

_____

_____

GOING DEEPER: 3 KEYS

What are 3 key learnings from this chapter? What are 3 key quotes or comments from the chapter that resonate with you? What are 3 key questions you now have? Thinking of your role as an educator, how does the information from this chapter cause you to think about your practice? In what ways does this information cause you to think differently about your school or district?

_____

_____

_____

_____

_____

_____

_____

_____

9

Institutionalizing Cultural Knowledge Through Collective Learning

Establishing knowledge sharing practices is as much a route to creating collaborative cultures as it is a product of the latter. This means that the organization must frame the giving and receiving of knowledge as a responsibility and must reinforce such sharing through incentives and opportunities to engage in it.

—Fullan, 2003, p. 86

Getting Centered

Institutionalizing cultural knowledge is an Essential Element of Cultural Proficiency that aligns well with Hord's (Hord & Sommers, 2008) attribute of collective learning and generative knowledge.

Coupled together they represent a powerful educational tool and the transformative nature of learning communities. In Chapter 8, we discussed how learning about our students as cultural entities is of major importance. Learning about our communities and the cultures within those communities extends and deepens our learning in ways that we educators benefit from personally and, as a result, we become more effective professionals.

As you read Michael Fullan's (2003) quote, what comes to mind for you? In what ways do you and your colleagues engage in learning about the cultural groups within your school community? Would you consider yourself to be culturally similar to or different from most of your students? Are most of the educators in your school culturally similar or different from your students? In what ways do community members share their cultural knowledge?

Please use the space below to record your comments.

_____

_____

_____

_____

Institutionalizing Cultural Knowledge

Culturally proficient learning communities recognize that our schools' curriculum and instructional programs work well for the students for whom they were designed—mostly middle-class, predominately white students. That reality is acknowledged for our historical successes in the public education systems in Canada and the United States and for its blindness to communities not included. Accordingly, culturally proficient learning communities engage one another in learning about the cultures and communities in their service areas.

The focus of culturally proficient learning communities transcends the heroes and holidays, or as Banks (1994) described, the "additive" approaches, and focuses on learning

- how best to communicate with various cultural groups,
- how best to problem solve with the cultural groups our schools serve, and
- how best to engage parents or guardians and community groups as partners in their students' education.

Consider the following questions as guides to knowing your community. While driving to school in the morning or away from school in the afternoon, do you always take the same route? Do you ever vary your way to or from school so you can view the neighborhoods where your students live? How much do you know about the communities that comprise your school attendance area? To what extent are you comfortable in the communities served by your school? Now, what will you do with what you are learning?

To *institutionalize* cultural knowledge describes the extent to which professional learning shapes policies and practices that meet the needs of a diverse community and the extent to which professional learning opportunities are encouraged, shared, and applied both in classrooms and throughout the school and the community for the purpose of improving student learning. Having student achievement as a priority can be institutionalized by

- identifying and addressing student needs and benchmarking success indicators and
- developing a continuous improvement inquiry model to assess progress toward clearly stated achievement goals.

Collective Learning and Generative Knowledge

Collective efficacy implies that together we can make a difference. As a community of learners, we know and understand the importance of working interdependently rather than independently. The structure of schools often determines the accessibility and proximity to our co-learners and colleagues. In professional learning communities, our focus is on what we determine to learn and how we will learn it in order to address student's learning needs. We determine how to arrange our classrooms, our schedules, and our instructional strategies in ways to better serve our students. We structure data collection and analysis to shape our curriculum, instruction, and assessment plans. Professional communities that are focused on learning know, understand, and use reflective practice as the feedback loop in the continuous process of assessing our students' needs, monitoring their progress, and planning our instructional practice to meet those identified needs. When we get stuck, we ask ourselves breakthrough questions to mediate our best thinking. And the cycle of continuous learning focuses on student achievement and improved instructional practice.

Going Deeper With Cultural Proficiency

This chapter continues the focus on the Essential Elements of Cultural Proficiency by emphasizing adapting to diversity and its relationships with the attribute of learning communities' supportive and shared conditions. Table 9.1 presents three lanes of information:

- The first column presents a description of institutionalizing cultural knowledge.
- The second column presents a description of collective learning and generative knowledge.
- The third column presents the interaction of the two sources of elements and poses questions and incomplete sentences to guide culturally proficient learning communities.

Take a moment to review the guiding questions and incomplete sentences in the third column of Table 9.1. What is your reaction to the guiding questions? Which questions guide your work at the school?

Table 9.1   Institutionalizing Cultural Knowledge Through Collective Learning and Generative Knowledge in Culturally Proficient Learning Communities

Institutionalizing Cultural Knowledge	*Collective Learning and Generative Knowledge*	*Questions to Guide Institutionalizing Cultural Knowledge Through Collective Learning and Generative Knowledge*
Extent to which professional learning shapes policies and practices that meet the needs of diverse learners. Professional learning opportunities are encouraged, shared, and applied in classrooms and throughout the school and the community for the purpose of improving student learning.	Community focus is on what the community determines to learn and how they will learn it in order to address student's learning needs.	• In what ways do I identify and address student needs by benchmarking success indicators? • In what ways do I develop and use a continuous improvement inquiry model to assess progress toward clearly stated achievement goals? • To keep myself informed, I have been reading . . . • To keep myself informed, I am engaged in this learning activity . . . • I bring cultural information to school in the form of . . . • I engage in inquiry to inform my thinking and behaviors to . . .

Which questions are present in the ongoing discussions among faculty and staff at your school? Which questions pose the opportunity for further learning for you and for your school? How do you respond to the incomplete sentences that ask how you engage and learn? The space below is for you to record your comments, thoughts, questions, and feelings.

_____

_____

_____

_____

Voices From the Field

Maple View School District provides two vignettes to illustrate the dynamics that surround institutionalizing cultural knowledge and collective learning and generative knowledge.

Vignette 9: Institutionalizing Professional Community, Learning

The Maple View School District, Elementary Schools Division, held their annual back-to-school staff development session prior to the opening of school. This year, the structure had changed from the traditional inservice day to a professional learning model. The Staff Development Department had taken on a new title, The Professional Learning Division. The assistant superintendent for Curriculum Development and Professional Learning is now using the National Staff Development Council (NSDC, 2001) Standards as guidelines for all professional learning sessions at the district office and at school sites.

The newly selected Professional Learning Planning Team designed the first day's session to include Professional Learning Leadership Teams (PLLTs) from each elementary school. The PLLTs would then design and develop a session for their own school sites based on their work with their administrative teams. This new focus shifted the traditional opening inservice days from individual learning to team-based and schoolwide learning. The focus of the professional learning was using the Tools for Cultural Proficiency to improve our teaching practices with a focus on improving achievement for all students.

Let's join one of the PLLTs as they discuss their experience using the Continuum post-it activity to assess cultural knowledge of themselves and their colleagues.

Melina (PLLT Chair):	This activity was really an eye-opener! When the facilitator described the first three points on the left side of the Continuum, I could hardly think of any examples from our school to write on my post-its. Could you guys?
Moses (fifth year teacher):	I had a hard time, too. I had lots of examples for the right side of the Continuum, though.
Kat (third year Principal):	Me, too. And did you notice how many post-its folks from other schools put up on the left side? That is the "unhealthy" side! Keep in mind, we've been working on our goals for Cultural Proficiency as part of our School Improvement Plan for the past three years. Remember when we first did the Continuum three years ago? We had lots of post-its on the left side.
Larry (veteran teacher):	So I guess I still am not so sure why I'm on this team. I've been at this school for more years than some of you have been alive (smile). We are the oldest school in the district and had the lowest school scores for two years before Kat came on as principal. Kat, when you encouraged me to be on this leadership team, I thought I must be crazy to accept this extra duty. When I watched what happened with the Continuum activity, I'm still not sure how we've made this much progress with the kids we have.
Moses:	Well, Larry, you are part of the reason. When Kat asked us at the first faculty meeting, "What are each of you willing to commit to, so we can improve our students' learning?" you stood up and said, "I'll need to learn more about today's kids." Her question and your response helped us all think about what we really knew or didn't know about our kids and the community. Kat called that *breakthrough thinking*, remember?

Breakthrough Questions

Creating a whole that is more than the sum of its parts may be a mathematical anomaly, but it certainly is descriptive of the synergy of successful learning teams. This dialogue of the PLLT provides opportunities for deepening the conversation in a manner that is indicative of culturally proficient learning communities. Successful learning teams strategically avoid getting stuck in a downward spiral of negative, difficult statements and questions that serve as barriers to moving forward to improve educational practice and pose breakthrough questions to address the statements and questions in Table 9.2. How might you pose breakthrough questions?

Table 9.2 Vignette 9: Instituting Professional Community, Learning

Barrier Statements and Questions	Breakthrough Questions
Consultant: *Knowing that the district goal is for all teachers to integrate these lessons into their curriculum, I have a concern as to how we might be more inclusive of others from the very beginning of our work.*	*In what ways have we successfully responded to initiatives in the past?*
Teacher: *Well, we could look at our students' data to see if the PBL lessons are having an impact on our students' success.*	*Your Breakthrough Question:*

REFLECTION

What might be some outcomes as a result of the team in providing professional learning for the faculty and entire school community? Who might be some other stakeholders the learning team might want to engage in this process? What are some guidelines you might use to identify who needs to be at the table? What other contexts might you consider for being more inclusive in decision making? Please record your responses in the space below.

_____

_____

_____

_____

Vignette 10: Collective Learning and Application

When the new team at Pine Hills High School proposed academies and pathways to the guidance department, the expected resistance melted. Some faculty were eager for opportunities to collaborate and share concerns about students and student work, as well as find ways to listen and talk with each other about challenges and successes with their own teaching and learning practices. Some faculty voiced concern to administrators, parents, and one another about the limited time available to discuss issues related to instruction and student work. The faculty wanted more involvement in decisions that might have an impact on them and their students. They were ready for organizational change. There was always time to do the mundane managerial type stuff that happened in staff meetings. Teachers on the Data Learning Team (DLT) and the administrators were meeting to discuss possible changes.

Rick (11th-grade veteran teacher):	What's this? This sounds like a conspiracy. Do they actually want to move us to different rooms on different parts of the campus? I've been in my room for over 21 years. I am not moving. I like being next to the library. Move? For what? In order to work with each other? I have trouble believing this.
Cynthia (fifth year, 10th-grade teacher):	Okay, Rick. Let's go with the flow. And now in our third year of the learning communities, I heard one of the teachers say this morning: "We must invite and bring all the English and math teachers to the same area on campus." Something about more opportunities for ideas to "bump into" others because of proximity? I just wanna know what being close to each other has to do with students? Could this be the *networking* I've been hearing about?
Aiden (new teacher):	OK, just hear me out. Last year we moved all the ninth-grade classrooms to the same wing. When our students move to our team member's classrooms for our flex time—you know, the flexibility grouping we've been doing—well, we teachers stand outside our classroom doors and greet the new students coming to our room. It's

	fun to chat and laugh with the kids and each other in the hallway—you know, just to get to know our kids better. It's working for us, anyway.
Juan (assistant principal):	That's a good example of how we are changing to meet the needs of our students. Maybe we can identify additional benefits for our students.
Lena (ninth year English teacher):	Yeah, we've noticed a decrease in tardies, even. I'd like to be able to share these data we've collected about our students and then talk about our next steps. What are some other ways we can share what is working and what isn't working for our students?

These kinds of conversations offer opportunities that nurture new ventures in instructional practices, especially when they talk about what's working and what's not working. Relocating classrooms to support team learning and student achievement is one way of disturbing the system. Beware! These intentional disturbances can lead to improved relationships, improved instructional strategies, and improved student achievement.

Prior to having their classes next door to each other at Pine Hills High School, teachers not in SLCs talked about how little they knew teachers from different disciplines. Now that they form interdisciplinary teams, they have begun to plan overlapping connected lessons together. New relationships have connected more of the school than ever before. Quickly, more and more information became available and changed the school's existing identity from noncaring to caring. There was an increase in attendance at the ninth-grade level in the first year of SLC implementation. Faculty talked about bumping into each other in their common planning periods. The bumping was through talking about information that they all wanted access to and the interpretation of this information to make decisions about their efforts, such as when they shared students' challenges and successes. Faculty compared notes on students whose grades had dropped in one class, but not in another. Faculty also discussed students who didn't get along with one teacher, but were at the top of their game in another class. The bumping happened when they called a student's home to speak with a parent and were able not only to get to know mom or dad, an uncle or aunt or grandparent, but also to talk about the student's strengths and the need to be involved in extracurricular activities with the parents. Teachers began to huddle in the hallways.

They met and planned how to increase the number of students passing math and ready for the next level. The counselors shared data that revealed too many students were entering ninth grade in need of pre-algebra. The Learning Team talked about the reasons for changing how classes would be scheduled based on student needs. They realized how important it had become to reflect and ask questions together.

Breakthrough Questions

Generative knowledge is often the result of explicit learning. In Vignette 10, the educators were interested in what they could learn about their students and the students' parents or guardians that would inform their teaching repertoires. Culturally proficient learning communities are intentional in learning about students' and parents' cultures. This vignette provides opportunities for deepening the conversation in a manner that is indicative of culturally proficient learning communities. In what ways did the learning team in this vignette strategically avoid getting stuck in a downward spiral of negative, difficult statements and questions that serve as barriers to moving forward to improve educational practice and pose breakthrough questions to address the statements and questions in Table 9.3. How might you pose additional breakthrough questions?

Table 9.3   Vignette 10: Institutionalizing Cultural Knowledge and Collective Learning and Generative Knowledge

Barrier Statements and Questions	Breakthrough Questions
Teacher #1: *Do they actually want to move us to different rooms on different parts of the campus? I've been in my room for over twenty-one years. I am not moving.*	Example: *In what ways do you see that you can provide teachers from other disciplines your perspectives on our students?*
Teacher #2: *More opportunities for ideas to "bump into" others because of proximity? What does our being "close to each other" have to do with students?*	*Your Breakthrough Question:*

REFLECTION

As you think about Vignette 10, what thoughts arise for you? In what ways does your school institutionalize learning in ways to provide generative knowledge? How do the experiences of Pine Hills High School Data Learning Team inform the work you are doing?

_____

_____

_____

_____

GOING DEEPER: 3 KEYS

What are 3 key learnings from this chapter? What are 3 key quotes or comments from the chapter that resonate with you? What are 3 key questions you now have? Thinking of your role as an educator, how does the information from this chapter cause you to think about your practice? In what ways does this information cause you to think differently about your school or district?

_____

_____

_____

_____

_____

_____

_____

_____

_____

PART III

Call to Action

Disturb the System
Through Curiosity and Inquiry

The final section of this book invites and supports you to access two new allies: curiosity and disturbance. We introduced these allies to you in the epigraph of Chapter 1 through the words of Margaret Wheatley:

> *Most people I meet want to develop more harmonious and satisfying relationships—in their organizations, communities, and personal lives. But we may not realize that this desire can only be satisfied by partnering with new and strange allies—curiosity and disturbance.*

> —Margaret Wheatley, 2001, p. 1

Chapters 1 through 9 added to your knowledge and raised your consciousness about learning communities. We introduced a different perspective on current PLC thinking by rearranging these familiar words to read PCL: professional communities, learning. We offered the conceptual frame of culturally proficient learning communities to integrate the Essential Elements of Cultural Proficiency with the tenets of learning communities. Maple View served as the context for authentic groups to use tools and strategies to actively engage in

- collectively inquiring and learning;
- sharing beliefs, values, vision, leadership and practice; and
- creating and sharing supportive conditions.

This frame for equitable teaching and learning is designed to support all students. Early on, we cautioned you that this book is best used in community with others focused on continuous improvement of schools. Now, in this final chapter we invite you to commit to action: Engage systematically and consistently with others to create an environment in which all learners experience success at levels higher than ever before. In Chapter 10, we provide rationale for our approach as well as protocols, templates, rubrics, and strategies to move the work forward. You will write the final words to this chapter. The question for you is this: In what ways am I willing to commit myself and my professional communities to use Cultural Proficiency as a lens through which we examine and design and/or redesign our current work?

10

Aligning Our Behaviors
With Our Values

*Moral purpose of the highest order is having a system where all
students learn, the gap between high and low performance becomes
greatly reduced, and what people learn enables them to be successful citizens and workers in a morally based knowledge society.*

—Fullan, 2003, p. 29

Getting Centered

As you read Michael Fullan's (2003) comment on moral purpose,
what comes to mind for you? What will it take to close the education
gap? In what ways do your actions align with your values? Are you
who you say you are? Do the actions of your colleagues align with the
core values stated in the organization's mission statement?

_____

_____

_____

_____

This book provides an integration of the Essential Elements of Cultural Proficiency and the tenets of professional learning communities. In Chapter 1, we presented our framework for understanding, analyzing, and sustaining Culturally Proficient Learning Communities (Table 1.1). The framework displays the Essential Elements of Cultural Proficiency alongside the tenets for professional learning communities. The third column characterizes culturally competent behaviors of learning community members. These behaviors are grounded in the core values of culturally proficient educational practices (Tool 2: The Guiding Principles). Without these deeply held values, individuals and learning teams will experience difficulty in achieving the ultimate goal of narrowing and closing the educational gap that Fullan (2003) describes in the opening epigraph of this chapter. Professional learning communities' work is *the work*; Cultural Proficiency is *the lens* through which the community views its work. Cultural Proficiency does not add a longer "to do" list to our current work. Cultural Proficiency enhances and deepens that work resulting in high achievement for all students.

Professional learning communities have evolved over the past 30 years from isolated classrooms of teachers-as-independent-contractors attending occasional faculty information meetings to today's professional educators participating in formal structures of professional learning communities for sharing ideas, strategies, vision, practice, resources, and results. As teaching shifts from a scope-and-sequence, compliance model to a standards and performance-based professional model, educators work collaboratively to design and develop grade-level assessments, instructional strategies, and appropriate curriculum. These collaborative efforts are intentional and research-based (Hord, 2008, June 1). We reiterate one of Hord's (2008, June 1) key questions: *What should we intentionally learn in order to become more effective in our teaching so that students learn well?* (p. 12).

Through our work with educators over the past 40 years, we offer the following opportunities to go deeper with your learning, your questions, your intentionality, and your actions.

Deepen Your Knowledge of the Culture of Your School and Community

The widely used and generally accepted definition of organizational culture is *the way we do things around here.* So often, educators continue to do things the way they've always done them because of the time and resources and energy required to do things differently. Current accountability measures have caused teachers and school leaders to question the ways things are done. Intentionally examining school culture requires teachers and leaders to ask: *What evidence do we have to confirm or deny that we act and behave in ways to support all learners?*

Teachers and school leaders who know and understand organizational culture realize education occurs within the social context of diversity, flexibility, complexity, and the contingency of situations. Having this worldview of teaching, learning, and leading educators can facilitate professional learning through inquiry. Below the surface of the behaviors and actions of members of an organization are the deeply held values, beliefs, and assumptions about how students learn. Asking questions to help surface those assumptions, collecting and analyzing student achievement data, and engaging in reciprocal, collaborative processes focused on all students experiencing success helps us dig deeply to explore the question: *Are we who we say we are?*

Deepen Your Knowledge of the Big Picture Through Systems Thinking

The typical organizational chart for school districts identifies roles and hierarchy by individual and departmental titles. Organizational members recognize the chart as representative of the formal structure of authority and chain of command. The chart does not, however, represent a true picture of informal leadership, relationships, information, communication flow, or sense of purpose within the organization. A visual depiction of the real life of the organization would be messy and nonlinear. Like people within the organization, schools are dynamic, multidimensional, highly complex, diverse, and ever changing. The twenty-first-century science of systems and complexity thinking helps us study schools as living systems with the ability to grow, self-organize, reorganize, and nurture themselves. Systems thinking helps us see order in seeming chaos and find simplicity in complex organizations as individuals come together around shared meaning, ideas, vision, purpose, resources, space, and information. This sharing phenomenon creates webs of collaboration and connections.

Culturally proficient learning communities recognize these connections as opportunities to assess cultural knowledge, value the diversity of the organization, manage the dynamics of diversity and complexity, adapt to changing environments and demographics, and institutionalize cultural knowledge through processes, procedures, policies, and practices. The entire system may, in fact, be too large for individuals or teams to impact, influence, or initiate change processes. However, systems respond to disturbances within the organization. Small disturbances can create large responses. For example, one parent group working with administrators at a school in a large, urban school district initiated changes in the school calendar. The response was so favorable from the parents and the data indicated such a positive effect on student attendance that the entire school district implemented the new school calendar. Parent involvement with school administrators became the leverage point to move the whole system forward.

Locate the Leverage Points

Leverage points function as places to enter the system to produce different or new outcomes. Leverage points, from systems thinking language, are also called *interventions* in school improvement language. These leverage points are opportunities to shift long-term behaviors from unhealthy patterns and negative outcomes to healthy, productive behaviors and positive outcomes. In *Culturally Proficient Inquiry* (Lindsey et al., 2008) our colleagues designed rubrics for four high-leverage interventions in schools:

- Curriculum and instruction
- Assessment and accountability
- Parent and community involvement
- Professional development and learning

Table 10.1 lists the five Essential Elements of Cultural Proficiency in the first column. Each of the columns to the right gives the extent to which the essential element might disturb the system through each of the leverage points. School leaders might use this table to help determine possible entry points for innovations and initiatives to positively impact student achievement for all students.

As you examine the rubrics, where might the leverage points be for you to enter the system for change in relation to your learning communities? In what ways might the essential elements serve to improve access issues for students, parents and guardians, and community partners?

Table 10.1   Leverage Points and the Five Essential Elements of Cultural Competence

Five Essential Elements	Leverage Points			
	Curriculum and Instruction	*Assessment*	*Parents and Community*	*Professional Development*
Valuing Diversity	Extent to which curriculum reflects diversity.	Extent to which cultural differences are used to gather data.	Extent to which parent and community diversity is valued.	Extent to which professional development addresses cultural issues.
Assessing Culture	Extent to which curriculum provides opportunities for educators and students to learn about self and others.	Extent to which disaggregated data are used to enhance knowledge and shape practice.	Extent to which community involvement facilitates the identification, assessment, and development of cultural identity.	Extent to which professional development addresses issues of cultural identity.
Managing the Dynamics of Difference	Extent to which curriculum promotes multiple perspectives.	Extent to which data is used to address the gaps between cultural groups.	Extent to which community involvement efforts develop the capacity to mediate cultural conflict between and among diverse parent/ community groups and the school.	Extent to which professional development promotes and models the use of inquiry and dialogue related to multiple perspectives and issues arising from diversity.

(Continued)

Table 10.1 (Continued)

| Five Essential Elements | Leverage Points | | | |
	Curriculum and Instruction	Assessment	Parents and Community	Professional Development
Adapting to Diversity	Extent to which cultural knowledge is integrated into the curriculum.	Extent to which assessments are changed to meet the needs of cultural groups.	Extent to which people and schools change to meet the needs of the community.	The extent to which professional learning facilitates change to meet the needs of the community.
Institutionalizing	Extent to which values and policies support culturally responsive curriculum.	Extent to which assessment data shapes values and policies to meet the needs of cultural groups.	Extent to which people and schools integrate knowledge about diverse community and organizational cultures into daily practice.	The extent to which professional development shapes policies and practices that meet the needs of a diverse community.

Source: From *Culturally Proficient Inquiry: A Lens for Identifying and Examining Educational Gaps,* by Randall B. Lindsey, Stephanie M. Graham, R. Chris Westphal, Jr., & Cynthia L. Jew, 2008, Thousand Oaks, CA: Corwin. Used with permission.

Deepen Your Knowledge of Culturally Proficient Educational Practices

The discussions, stories, planning, and authors' experiences generated and presented in this book are fractal-like. They are steeped in layers of details and design, bifurcated relationships, and iterative patterns of connectedness. They are anchored in something that might be called *learning fractals.* University of California at Los Angles's Merle Wittrock suggested to us in 1974 that learning is generative. Some of this book's thinking captures aspects of generative learning, particularly as we show an inevitable entanglement of prior understandings and beliefs with new concepts, experiences, and learnings. The resulting resistance to accepting emerging learnings is foundational for taking different actions that impact organizational growth. This growth happens through layers of minute and multiple opportunities of high impact change.

The stories we educators dare to share tell the lives of our organizations and communities. Without them, we deny ourselves the knowing of each other that brings us deeper appreciation for what we know now that was not known prior to our sharing. Critical learning is seated in personal meaning and personal experiences that bring *inside-out* thinking to the surface. Many of us know that learning about one's self can be a revelation as well as a transforming experience. What does it take for us to realize that when such learning happens simultaneously within a group, an organization, or a community that the experience is often profound? Such learnings necessitate incredible dimensions. That is, they are multileveled and simultaneously happening on both a small scale and a large scale. They are process-oriented, layered, patterned experiences. Such details and experiences create learning images or learning fractals.

Learning communities by their very nature are issues-based, reflective, diverse, and interconnected through inquiry. With growth, these communities are in a constant state of chaos, finding themselves and self-organizing. This is only part of their complexity. Such complexity is one of the lifelines to learning fractals.

For us to notice each other's thinking is not enough; what we *choose to do* with what we notice and how we use feedback can strategically make a difference in our lives. Investing time to build relationships often provides the stickiness that sustains and shoulders layers of surprise, complexity, fear, and uncertainty in our personal and organizational lives. Communities that learn and grow do so by choice—the choice to do something that makes a difference with the learning by intention and design. How we use that learning to move our communities and ourselves forward is critical. Learning is an opportunity for exploring, rediscovering who we are, knowing where and how we might continue our multidestinational journey in life, finding fun, expecting surprises, and finding hope for our children and grandchildren's futures.

Call to Action

Understanding the power and potential of *culturally proficient professional communities, learning* to impact teaching and learning may be the single most important information school leaders need in today's complex learning environments. The single most important skill for educational leaders is to balance investigation and inquiry for the purpose of improving student achievement with the planning and implementing of new programs. Creating a culturally proficient school culture supports collective inquiry for the purpose of all students' learning.

Often, new programs are mandated at the governance level and implemented at school sites within months. This reflexive response is well documented through NCLB mandates, state-required programs, and government-monitored processes. New programs are implemented as if each were the answer for which all educators have been waiting. Little time or attention is given for educators to think about their own thinking. Before viewing new programs as the *answer*, perhaps school leaders should first inquire, *What was the question?*

No doubt, we live in data-rich educational environments. Perhaps our new work is not in collecting more data, but in asking questions to determine what data are needed and how we will examine those data in ways to impact our instructional practice. Culturally proficient learning communities work with students and their families, teachers, and leaders to find useful data and help make meaning of the data for the benefit of all students. Rather than looking for the right answers, maybe we need to ask the right questions. What are we curious about? What are we willing to do to make the difference? For what are we waiting?

Your Turn: Intentionally Designing Curiosity and Disturbance

Now, it is your turn. First, think about the questions that you typically ask. Think about the questions you typically hear from your colleagues. Write some of those questions in the blank spaces in Table 10.2.

Table 10.2 What Questions Do We Ask?

Curiosity: What Questions Do We Ask?
1.
2.
3.
4.
5.

Once you've written the usual questions you ask and hear in Table 10.2, think about what you expected the answers to be. What results did you expect, predict, or actually receive in response to those questions? Write your responses in the blank spaces in Table 10.3.

Table 10.3   What Results Did We Expect or Find?

Disturbances: What Are the Results or Outcomes of Our Questions?
1.
2.
3.
4.
5.

Take a look at the questions and the anticipated or actual results you wrote in Table 10.2 and Table 10.3. What do you notice? What patterns or themes do you see? Write your responses in the blank spaces in Table 10.4.

Table 10.4   Patterns or Themes From Our Questions and Responses

What Are the Patterns or Themes of Our Questions and Our Results/Outcomes?
1.
2.
3.
4.

REFLECTION

As you look at the information from Table 10.2 through Table 10.4, what are you thinking? What might be some of the conditions that influence the kinds of questions you and your colleagues ask? Do the results of your questions match what you predicted would happen?

Write your reflective thoughts in the spaces below.

_____

_____

_____

_____

Choose Your Questions

As learning community members, we have the opportunity to choose the questions we ask. Which questions serve us best in times of change and transition? Are our questions mediating thinking and progress toward our desired results, or are our questions creating barriers to thinking and progress? Dr. Marilee G. Adams, author of *Change Your Questions, Change Your Life* (2004), writes:

> . . . we build our worlds with our questions, and creating real change and new possibilities requires asking new ones, both of ourselves and each other. (p. 174)

Adams is the originator of QuestionThinking™, a set of tools to foster inquiry and productivity. Her model has helped forward the work of transformational leaders, productive teams, and inquiring organizations. The model is grounded in the psychology of how words shape our thinking. For example, questions will influence our thoughts, feelings, and behaviors (Adams, 2004). From the often-used phrase *mind over matter* to the well-know children's book, *The Little Engine That Could*, the relation of words to thoughts and actions has guided educators for many years. Therefore, it makes sense that our questions may, in fact, help us do our best thinking, which will lead to desired outcomes and results. We applied Adam's model and Costa and Garmston's (1994) question protocols used by cognitive coaches to mediate the thinking of teachers and school leaders to develop our breakthrough questions used in Chapters 5 through 9. Table 10.5 displays the two types of questions we have labeled *barrier questions* and *breakthrough questions*. The use of barrier questions will

- shut down thinking,
- assign judgment,
- focus on blame, and
- attack or intimidate other members of the group.

Whereas, the use of breakthrough questions will

- encourage thoughtful responses,
- redirect negative thinking toward positive responses,
- invite flexibility,
- generate both-and thinking,
- consider other's experiences and perspectives,
- invite possibility and creative thinking,
- value differences, and
- create cognitive shifts in thinking.

Table 10.5 Barriers and Breakthroughs for Thinking

We have the opportunity to choose our questions:

- When an answer is given to us, what questions might we ask?
- Which questions serve us best in times of transition?

What questions are we asking?

Barrier Questions	Breakthrough Questions
What is wrong?	What is working?
Whose fault is this?	For what am I (are we) responsible?
How do I prove that it's not my fault?	What (facts) got us to this situation?
How can I protect my interests and turf?	What is best for the community?
How can I control the situation?	What choices/opportunities do I/we have?
What is at stake for me?	What's helpful/useful for me/us to know and do?
How will this hurt me?	What might I learn from this?
Why don't they get it?	What might they be feeling, needing, and wanting?
Why even bother with this?	Now, what is possible?

Characteristics of Culturally Proficient Breakthrough Questions

Breakthrough questions serve the learning community by introducing new curiosities and time to think. Just by asking these thinking questions, new possibilities emerge. Integrating skills for asking mediational questions with the Tools for Cultural Proficiency produces culturally proficient breakthrough questions. Effective culturally proficient breakthrough questions

- use the essence of one or more of the Essential Elements of Cultural Proficiency to shape the action in the question;
- use exploratory, plural, and inclusive language;
- use positive intentionality;

- use language to mediate thinking and/or action toward goals; and
- use language that redirects thinking from certainty to curiosity and possibility.

As you examine Table 10.5, think about the questions you typically ask. Look back at your responses in Table 10.2. Are they barrier or breakthrough questions, or a mixture of the two types? Which type produced positive results for you and your learning communities?

Cultural Proficiency *is* breakthrough thinking. It is a mindset focused on individual behaviors and organizational policies and procedures that support cross-cultural communication. Cultural Proficiency may also represent a shift in thinking from tolerance for diversity to transformational thinking and behaviors. This shift in thinking can be motivated and supported by asking breakthrough questions, as you and the characters from Maple View did in the earlier chapters in this book. Table 10.6 lists examples of breakthrough questions for culturally proficient change and action. Take a minute to examine the questions. How might these questions guide your work and the work of your learning communities?

Table 10.6 Breakthrough Questions for Culturally Proficient Change

- What do I want for myself and for others related to this change initiative?
- What are my choices related to this initiative?
- What assumptions do I, and others in my community, hold about this change initiative?
- For what am I responsible related to this initiative?
- What might be other ways that I can think about this initiative?
- What are my colleagues and community members thinking, feeling, needing, and wanting in regard to this initiative?
- What might be some things I'm missing, not hearing, or not seeing related to this initiative?
- What might be some things I will learn from the experts, from mistakes, and from successes?
- What questions am I, and are we, asking?
- What are some action steps that make the most sense at this stage of the initiative?
- How might we view this initiative as a win-win opportunity?
- Who else might need to be involved in our change initiative conversations and decisions?
- Now, what is possible?

Source: Reprinted with permission of the publisher. From *Change Your Questions, Change Your Life,* copyright © 2004 by Marilee Adams, Berrett-Koehler Publishers, Inc., San Francisco, CA. All rights reserved. www.bkconnection.com

Your Turn

Will the questions you typically ask produce the results or outcomes you have set as your goals? Table 10.7 provides an Action Plan template to help you analyze the potential of the questions you ask. Use the breakthrough questions in Tables 10.5 and 10.6 and the Characteristics of Culturally Proficient Breakthrough questions to help you construct your culturally proficient breakthrough action questions.

Table 10.7   Breakthrough Questions Lead to Desired Results

What Might Be Our Breakthrough, Action Questions?	What Results Do We Anticipate?	Who Takes the Lead?	Who Else Needs to Be Involved/Invited?	What Results/Outcomes Did We Achieve?

Final Reflections, Questions, and Actions

As you reflect on the content of this book, what comes to mind for you? The following questions intentionally use the personal pronoun *I* so you might use these questions to guide your thinking and planning:

What am I most intentional about in my teaching and learning?

_____

_____

Who am I, in relation to my colleagues?

_____

_____

Who are we as a professional community?

_____

_____

What are we learning?

_____

_____

What do we do with what we learn?

_____

_____

Who else do we need to include in our professional community?

_____

_____

What additional data would be helpful to us as we develop our learning goals?

_____

_____

The final words of this book will be yours. Space is provided for you to commit to actions steps. These final questions are designed to help you focus on your future actions and commitment to yourself and your learning community:

- In what ways am I willing to commit myself to the use of Cultural Proficiency as a lens through which I examine and design or redesign my current work?
- In what ways am I willing to commit my learning communities to the use of Cultural Proficiency as a lens through which we examine and design or redesign our current work?
- What are my short- and long-term goals? What will I/we accomplish with our commitment to this work?
- What are the first steps I will take?

Use this space to record your responses and your commitments.

_____

_____

_____

_____

Our Invitation and Commitment to You

We are partners with you in this journey toward culturally proficient educational practices. We invite you to engage with us about your experiences as a member of a professional learning community. We'd like to hear your stories, your questions, and your commitments to this work. Please share your strategies, your learning, your actions, and your materials as you explore curiosities and disturb the systems in which you work. We look forward to conversation with you.

Contact us:

Delores is at dblindsey@aol.com

Linda is at ljungwirth@conveningconversations.com

Jarvis is at jarvispahl@juno.com

Randy is at randallblindsey@aol.com

References

Adams, Marilee. (2004). *Change your questions, change your life: 7 powerful tools for life and work*. San Francisco: Berrett-Koehler.

Banks, James. (1994). *Multiethnic education: Theory and practice*. Needham, MA: Allyn & Bacon.

Bardwick, Judith. (1996). *In praise of good business*. New York: John Wiley & Sons.

Barth, Roland. (1991). *Improving schools from within: Teachers, parents, and principals can make the difference*. New York: John Wiley & Sons.

Berliner, David C. (2006). Our impoverished view of educational reform. *Teachers College Record, 108*(6), 949–995.

Berman, Paul, McLaughlin, Milbrey, Bass-Golod, Gail, Pauly, Edward, & Zellman, Gail. (1977). *Federal programs supporting educational change, Vol. VII: Factors affecting implementation and continuation* (Report No. R-1589/7-HEW). Santa Monica, CA: Rand. (ERIC Document Reproduction Service No. ED140 432)

Bracey, Gerald. (2006). Sixteenth Bracey report on the condition of public education. *Phi Delta Kappan, 17*, 15.

Buenida, Edward, Ares, Nancy, Juarez, Brenda, & Peercy, Megan. (2004, Winter). The geographies of difference: The production of east side, west side, and central city school. *American Educational Research Journal, 41*(4), 833–863.

Comer, James P. (1988). Educating poor and minority children. *Scientific American, 259*(5), 42–48.

Costa, Arthur, & Garmston, Robert. (1994). *Cognitive Coaching: A foundation for renaissance schools*. Norwood, MA: Christopher-Gordon.

Cotton, Kathleen. (1996). *School size, school climate, and student performance: Close-up #20*. Portland, OR: Northwest Regional Educational Laboratory. Retrieved June 9, 2008, from http://www.nwrel.org/scpd/sirs/10/c020.html

Covey, Stephen R. (2004). *The Seven Habits of Highly Effective People: Restoring the Character Ethic*. New York: Free Press.

Cross, Terry. (1989). *Toward a culturally competent system of care*. Washington, DC: Georgetown University Child Development Program, Child and Adolescent Service System Program.

DuFour, Richard, & Eaker, Robert. (1998). *Professional learning communities at work: Best practices for enhancing student achievement*. Alexandria, VA: Association for Supervision and Curriculum Development.

Eaker, Robert. (2004). A focus on learning. In The National Educational Service's Seventh Annual Institute, *Professional learning communities at work: Best practices for enhancing student achievement* (pp. 225–231). Bloomington, IN: National Educational Service.

Edmonds, Ronald. (1979). Some schools work and more can. *Social Policy, 9*(5), 3.

Fuhrman, Susan, & Elmore, Richard. (2004). *Redesigning accountability systems for education.* New York: Teachers College Press.

Fullan, Michael. (1999). *Change forces: The sequel.* London: Falmer Press.

Fullan, Michael. (2003). *The moral imperative of school leadership.* Thousand Oaks, CA: Corwin.

Garmston, Robert, & Wellman, Bruce. (2008). *The adaptive school: Developing and facilitating collaborative groups syllabus* (5th ed.). Norwood, MA: Christopher-Gordon.

Gay, Geneva. (2000). *Culturally responsive teaching: Theory, practice and research.* New York: Teachers College Press.

Goals 2000: Educate America Act. Washington, D.C.: U.S. Congress. http://www.ed.gov/legislation/GOALS2000/TheAct/index.html - accessed June 5, 2009

Hawley, Willis. (1983). *Strategies for effective desegregation: Lessons from research.* Lexington, MA: Lexington Books.

Heifetz, Ronald. (1994). *Leadership without easy answers.* Cambridge, MA: Belknap Press.

Hilliard, Asa. (1991). Do we have the will to educate all children? *Educational Leadership, 40*(1), 31–36.

hooks, bell. (1990). *Yearning: Race, gender and cultural politics.* Boston: South End Press.

Hord, Shirley M. (1992). *Facilitative leadership: The imperative for change.* Austin, TX: Southwest Educational Development Laboratory. Retrieved February 11, 2005, from http://www.sedl.org/change/facilitate/welcome.html

Hord, Shirley M. (1997). *Professional learning communities: Communities of continuous inquiry and improvement.* Austin, TX: Southwest Educational Development Laboratory.

Hord, Shirley M. (2008, June 1). Evolution of the professional learning community: Revolutionary concept is based on intentional collegial learning. *Journal of Staff Development, 29*(3), 6–12.

Hord, Shirley M., & Sommers, William L. (2008). *Leading professional learning communities: Voices from research and practice.* Thousand Oaks, CA: Corwin.

Kegan, Robert, & Lahey, Lisa Laskow. (2001). *How the way we talk can change the way we work: Seven languages for transformation.* San Francisco: Jossey-Bass.

Kotelnikov, Vadim. (2005). *Corporate vision, mission, goals, and strategies: Traditional and new approaches.* Retrieved March 14, 2005, from http://www.1000ventures.com/business_guide/crosscuttings/vision_mission_strategy.html

Kozol, Jonathan. (1991). *Savage inequalities: Children in America's schools.* New York: Harper Perennial.

Kozol, Jonathan. (2005). *The shame of a nation.* New York: Crown.

Kozol, Jonathan. (2007). *Letters to a young teacher.* New York: Crown.

Ladson-Billings, Gloria. (2005). *Beyond the big house: African American educators on teacher education.* New York: Teachers College Press.

Levin, Henry M. (1988). *Accelerated schools for at-risk students.* New Brunswick, NJ: Center for Policy Research in Education.

Lezotte, Lawrence. (1997). *Learning for all.* Okemos, MI: Effective Schools Products.

Lindsey, Delores, Martinez, Richard, & Lindsey, Randall. (2007). *Culturally proficient coaching.* Thousand Oaks, CA: Corwin.

Lindsey, Randall, Graham, Stephanie, Westphal, R. Chris, & Jew, Cynthia. (2008). *Culturally proficient inquiry: A lens for identifying and examining educational gaps.* Thousand Oaks, CA: Corwin.

Lindsey, Randall, Nuri Robins, Kikanza, & Terrell, Raymond. (2003). *Cultural proficiency: A manual for school leaders* (2nd ed.). Thousand Oaks, CA: Corwin.

Louis, Karen Seashore, & Kruse, Sharon D. (1995). *Professionalism in community: Perspectives on reforming urban schools.* Thousand Oaks, CA: Corwin.

McLaughlin, Milbrey W. (1990). The Rand change agent study revisited: Micro realities. *Educational Researcher, 19*(9), (pp. 11–16).

National Commission on Excellence in Education. (1983). *A nation at risk: The imperative for educational reform.* Retrieved March 14, 2005, from http://www.ed.gov/pubs/NatAtRisk/title.html

National Staff Development Council. (2001). *Standards for Staff Development.* Retrieved March 14, 2005, from http://nsdc.org/standards/index.cfm

Nieto, Sonia. (2004). *Affirming diversity: The sociopolitical context of multicultural education* (4th ed.). Boston: Pearson.

No Child Left Behind Act of 2001, P. L. 107–110. 107th Cong. Retrieved January 25, 2005, from http://www.ed.gov/policy/elsec/leg/esea02/index.html

Nuri Robins, Kikanza, Lindsey, Randall, Lindsey, Delores, & Terrell, Raymond. (2006). *Culturally proficient instruction: A guide for people who teach* (2nd ed.). Thousand Oaks, CA: Corwin.

Orfield, Gary, & Frankenberg, Elizabeth. (2007). *Lessons in integration: Realizing the promise of racial diversity in America's public schools.* Charlottesville: University of Virginia Press.

Owens, Robert G. (1995). *Organizational behavior in education* (5th ed.). Boston: Allyn & Bacon.

Oxley, Diana. (2001). *Small learning communities: A review of the research.* Philadelphia, PA: The Mid-Atlantic Regional Educational Laboratory Temple University Center for Research in Human Development and Education. Retrieved June 9, 2008, from http://www.temple.edu/lss/pdf/ReviewOfTheResearchOxley.pdf

Perie, Marianne, Moran, Rebecca, & Lutkus, Anthony D. (2005). *NAEP 2004 trends in academic progress: Three decades of student performance in reading and mathematics (NCES 2005–464).* U.S. Department of Education, Institute of Education Sciences, National Center for Education Statistics. Washington, D.C.: Government Printing Office.

Public School Accountability Act of 1999. CA. SBX1 1. (April 5). Retrieved March 30, 2009, from http://www.cde.ca.gov/ta/ac/pa/overview.asp

Ravitch, Diane. (2003). *A Nation at risk: Twenty years later.* Hoover Institution. Retrieved May 7, 2008, from http://www.hoover.org/pubaffairs/daily report/archive/2848976.html

Raywid, Mary Anne. (1996). *Taking stock: The movement to create mini-schools, schools-within-schools, and separate small schools.* New York: Columbia University, Teachers College, ERIC Clearinghouse on Urban Education.

Sadker, Myra, & Sadker, David. (1994). *Failing at fairness: How America's schools cheat girls.* New York: Charles Scribner's Sons.

Schmoker, Mike. (2006). *Results now.* Alexandria, VA: Association for Supervision and Curriculum Development.

Senge, Peter. (1990). *The fifth discipline: The art and practice of the learning organization.* New York: Doubleday/Currency.

Senge, Peter, Cambron-McCabe, Nelda, Lucas, Timothy, Smith, Bryan, Dutton, Janis, & Kleiner, Art. (2000). *Schools that learn: A fifth discipline fieldbook for educators, parents, and everyone who cares about education.* New York: Doubleday.

Sergiovanni, Thomas J. (1991). *The principalship: A reflective practice perspective.* Boston: Allyn & Bacon.

Sizer, Theodore R. (1985). *Horace's compromise: The dilemma of the American high school.* Boston: Houghton Mifflin.

Slavin, Robert. (1990). *Cooperative learning: Theory, research and practice.* Englewood Cliffs, NJ: Prentice Hall.

Slavin, Robert. (1996). *Every child, every school: Success for all.* Thousand Oaks, CA: Corwin.

Smylie, Mark A. (1995). Teacher learning in the workplace: Implications for school reform. In Thomas R. Guskey & Michael Huberman (Eds.), *Professional development in education: New paradigms & practices* (pp. 92–113). New York: Teachers College Press.

Takaki, Ronald. (2008). *A different mirror: A history of multicultural America.* New York: Back Bay Books, Little, Brown, and Company.

Terrell, Raymond D., & Lindsey, Randall B. (2009). *Culturally proficient leadership: The personal journey begins within.* Thousand Oaks, CA: Corwin.

Wartell, Michael A., & Huelskamp, Robert M. (1991, July 18). Testimony of Michael A. Wartell and Robert M. Huelskamp, Sandia National Laboratories, Before Subcommittee on Elementary, Secondary, and Vocational Education, Committee on Education and Labor, U.S. House of Representatives.

Wenger, Etienne. (1998). *Communities of practice: Learning, meaning, and identity.* New York: Cambridge University.

Wenger, Etienne, McDermott, Richard, & Snyder, William. (2002). *Cultivating communities of practice: A guide to managing knowledge.* Boston: Harvard Business School Press.

Wheatley, Margaret. (2001). *Disturb me, please!* Provo, Utah: Berkana Institute.

Wittrock, Merle C. (1974). A generative model of mathematics learning. *Journal for Research in Mathematics Education, 5*(4), 181–196.

Zellermayer, Michael, & Margolin, Ilana. (2005). Teacher educators' professional learning described through the lens of complexity theory. *Teachers College Record, 107*(6), 1275–1304. Retrieved October, 31, 2007, from http://www.tcrecord.org ID Number: 11911

Suggested Additional Reading

Boyd, Victoria, & Hord, Shirley. (1994). Schools as learning communities. *Issues . . . About Change, 4*(1). Retrieved May 28, 2008, from http://www.sedl.org/change/issues/issues41.html

Delpit, Lisa. (1995) *Other people's children: Cultural conflict in the classroom.* New York: The New Press.

Hall, Gene E., & Hord, Shirley M. (1987). *Change in schools: Facilitating the process.* Albany, NY: State University of New York Press.

Hord, Shirley M., Rutherford, William L., Huling-Austin, Leslie, & Hall, Gene. (1987). *Taking charge of change.* Alexandria, VA: Association for Supervision and Curriculum Development.

Kunjufu, Jawanza. (2002). *Black students–Middle-class teachers.* Chicago: African American Images.

Lindsey, Randall, Roberts, Laraine, & CampbellJones, Franklin. (2005). *The culturally proficient school: An implementation guide for school leaders.* Thousand Oaks, CA: Corwin.

McLaughlin, Milbrey W., & Berman, Paul. (1977). *The art of retooling educational staff development in a period of retrenchment.* Santa Monica, CA: RAND Corporation.

Schein, Edgar H. (1997). *Organizational culture and leadership* (2nd ed.). San Francisco: Jossey-Bass.

Weick, Karl. (1995). *Sensemaking in organizations.* Thousand Oaks, CA: Sage.

Index

CORWIN
A SAGE Company

The Corwin logo—a raven striding across an open book—represents the union of courage and learning. Corwin is committed to improving education for all learners by publishing books and other professional development resources for those serving the field of PreK–12 education. By providing practical, hands-on materials, Corwin continues to carry out the promise of its motto: **"Helping Educators Do Their Work Better."**